Outdoor Celebrities
COOKBOOK

RECIPES & OUTDOOR TALES FROM
AMERICA'S PREMIER OUTDOORS PEOPLE

JERRY MARTIN

BILL JORDAN

KEITH KAVAJECZ

MARK DRURY

— *BY BILL COOPER*

By Billie R. Cooper

Additional copies may be obtained at the cost of $21.95, plus $3.00 postage and handling, each book.

Missouri residents add $1.37 sales tax, each book.

Send to:

Billie R. Cooper
19255 St. Rt. EE
St. James, MO 65559

First Printing—November 1999

ISBN 0-9672035-0-3
LCCCN 99-093256

Then God said, *"Let the waters teem with fish and other life, and let the skies be filled with birds of every kind."*

⌒

And God said, *"Let the earth bring forth every kind of animal..."*

⌒

Then God said, *"Let us make a man—someone like ourselves, to be the master of all life upon the earth and in the skies and in the seas."*

Genesis 1:20, 24, 26

⌒

"A lazy man won't even dress the game he gets while hunting, but the diligent man makes good use of everything he finds."

Proverbs 12:27

"Now this is what we believe.
The Mother of us all is Earth.
The Father is the Sun.
The Grandfather is the Creator
Who bathed us with his mind
And gave life to all things.
The Brother is the
beast and trees.
The Sister is that with wings.
We are the Children of Earth.
And do it no harm in any way.
Nor do we offend the Sun
By not greeting it at dawn.
We praise our
Grandfather for his creation.
We share the same
breath together -
The beasts, the trees
The birds, the man."

Nancy Woods (Taos Indians)

The celebration of food, captured from wild environs and presented to family groups and tribes, was what defined Homosapiens, the human animal. Some 35 million years ago, evolution separated out a line from other human-like want-to-bes, ultimately becoming modern man.

Archaeologists, anthropologists, and paleontologists believe the use of tools was the turning point for the human line. I disagree. It wasn't tools, but food, and the wonderful family and tribal rituals which evolved around the capture of prey; return of successful hunters to the family and tribe; and the camaraderie associated with the preparation and consumption of wild foods.

Although separated by millions of years and all the accouterments of modern man, we still celebrate the act of hunting and killing of game, and the return of the successful hunter to the family by the preparation of the bountiful harvest. In our world, expert and artful preparation of fish and wildlife has replaced simple roasting over the communal fire, yet the symbols and psychological response of the soul to the wild foods still rings true. It is this connection to our ancestors which drives hunters and anglers to seek new and better ways to prepare the harvest.

Hunters and anglers were the original conservationists, protectors of our rich environmental heritage. Through the efforts of sportsmen, millions of acres of national and state park lands, refuges, and hunting lands have been set aside for future generations; and deer, turkey, beaver, waterfowl, and a host of other animals have been brought back from the brink of extinction. The simple act of purchasing a hunting and fishing license allows states to protect millions of acres of land from development and fight pollution of our streams and rivers; develop successful state and federal management philosophies to protect and conserve our rich wildlife heritage; and restore numerous wildlife populations across this wonderful country.

Hunters and anglers celebrate annually this wonderful gift passed down from our ancestors by participating in the ritual preparation of wild game, renewing once again our inner being.

The recipes presented by author Bill Cooper in the *Outdoor Celebrities Cookbook* are food for the body and food for the soul. Celebrity hunters and anglers, known locally and nationally who enjoy well prepared wild foods, share their special and once secret wildlife recipes, and those defining moments with family and friends spawned by preparation of wild foods. Enjoy the wondrous harvest from the fields and waters, the simple gastronomical delight of well prepared wild fish and game, and celebrate this rich heritage handed down from our ancestors.

Spence Turner

ACKNOWLEDGEMENTS

Thanks first and foremost to my constant and favorite outdoor companion, my wife, Charlene. Without her, this book would still be just an idea. She typed the manuscript, hounded people relentlessly for recipes, bios, and pictures, and most importantly, believed in the idea.

Thanks to my mother, Pauline Cooper, who proofread every recipe.

Thanks to David Besenger for the artwork and all those who provided outstanding photos for cover usage.

Thanks to those who provided stories and quotes: Bill Jordan, Joel Vance, Brad Harris, Michael Pearce, Mark Van Patten, Charles Waterman, and Charlie Farmer.

Thanks to Spence Turner for the introduction.

And thanks to the Creator for our great outdoors!

Bill Cooper

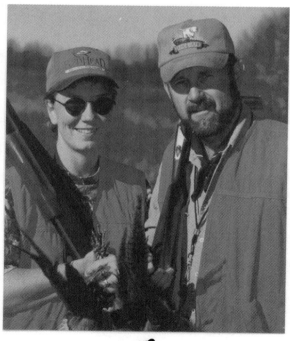

ENJOYING OUTDOOR FELLOWSHIP

We Americans love the outdoors. Our combined efforts have had dramatic effects on fish and wildlife populations in the United States. License fees paid by hunters and fishermen paved the way for vast conservation efforts. Deer and wild turkey returned to our woods, waterfowl to our skies, and fish to our lakes and streams.

An integral part of the conservation efforts in this country is the comradarie shared by outdoorsmen. The great outdoors is at the heart of the fellowship.

I was practically born outside, in the swamps of Mississippi County, Missouri. Our old family farmhouse of oak and cypress boards and tar paper covering allowed cold and critters free entry. Critters were the constant center of family discussion. We loathed the ones that made their way inside and loved the ones that preferred to stay outside, wild and free. Most of those we hunted.

Fortunately, we did our fishing outside, too. More than once, however, the Mississippi River backwaters lapped at our back door, threatening to move our carp gigging sessions indoors.

Hunting and fishing elevated our every day lives above the hard and often monotonous, agonizing farm labor. Hunting and fishing offered outdoor recreation in the purest form, an activity engaged in solely for the enjoyment derived from it. We came away from each trip recreated, refreshed, and happy. And more often than not we enjoyed a sumptuous meal made from our catch or kill.

Youngsters longed to become a part of the hunting and fishing excursions enjoyed by the older boys and men. When the time came for a youngster to tag along, a rite of passage took place that everyone understood. Unwritten rules verbally passed from one generation to the next while companions floated in a boat or listened to a running hound. Excitements and fears were shared. Stories were told and retold around campfires and kitchen tables.

The fellowship associated with outdoor affairs became addicting, necessary. The acceptance by those more experienced was heavy stuff for a kid. Forty years later, I still value those same experiences - enjoying a duck hunt with a new found friend or floating a stream with an old friend for the fiftieth time or comparing stories with a fellow outdoor writer, or best of all, ushering a kid through the rites of passage. And the tradition of outdoor fellowship lives on.

Bill Cooper

OUTDOOR FREEDOMS
AND THE FUTURE

I consider myself one of the luckiest people on earth. Never in our history has there been available so many outdoor opportunities to the common man of America. One might argue that the early pioneers had more hunting and fishing opportunities than we do today. Perhaps. However, pioneers were hardly common. And, most settled or homesteaded in an area where they spent the rest of their days.

Today's common man is extremely mobile. Federal and state fish and game agencies, headed by professional biologists, are in their prime. In my lifetime I have seen the return of the deer and wild turkey. Our streams are cleaner than when I was a kid. Regulations and sensible seasons have improved our fisheries, including many in our coastal waters.

I have caught trout in the cold, clear streams of the Appalachians, the Ozarks, and the Rockies, and fished for bass from Canada to Florida. I have chased quail from Missouri to south Texas and I have hunted, fished, floated, backpacked and explored dozens of beautiful places across our United States.

The people I have met and the outdoor meals I have enjoyed stick out in my mind as much as the places visited and game pursued. The hospitality of a south Texan, with whom I shared a splendid quail hunt, is remembered as is the young lady in Canada who hauled Charlene and me and our gear, by motorboat, to the Quetico Wilderness Area. An Arkansas duck blind, an Iowa pheasant field, a river camp on the Ozarks' Current River, a rafting trip down the Colorado, a mountain camp in Yellowstone—they all have been shared with people who treasure the same wild places as me.

Take all this for granted? No way! We have never had it so good in this country and few people around the world know the outdoor pleasures we enjoy.

During the colonial days, hunting and fishing were the most usual form of enjoying the outdoors, yet these pleasures were restricted in some areas. Puritanical thinking allowed the blood sports only in so far as they were necessary for livelihood. As pastimes, they were considered undesirable.

Upper classes, who clung to English tradition, enjoyed hunting and fishing as "sports." The "Fishhouse" in Philadelphia still exists today. Established in 1732, the Schuylkill Fishing Company of the state provided gardens and groves where men and women gathered to "divert themselves with fishing, walking, boating, and sleighing."

Southern tradition is steeped in deer hunting, wild fowl shooting, and riding after hounds. Every southern gentleman's social life included fox hunting. Even George Washington enjoyed following his swift French hounds.

In the North, fishing parties were leisure-time pleasures. In general, hunting and fishing for sport were recreational pursuits of the upper level society. The ordinary citizen did not indulge in such sports, and the conservative minded considered them a waste of time.

Writings from the period promoted the idea that sports were not fit for a Christian and businessmen regarded outdoor sports as frivolous pastimes of irresponsible young men. More than one publication stated that "hunting and fishing for mere sport, can never be justified."

By the end of the eighteenth century, in spite of the prejudices, some people regarded the outdoor sports of hunting and fishing as beneficial. The progressive Benjamin Franklin believed the outdoor sports to be healthy pastimes that calmed a person's temper and made him more pleasant and useful to society.

The periodical *American Forever* was one of the first to further the cause of hunting and fishing. Lines similar to the following were common:

Come, thou harmless recreation
Holding out the angler's reed,
Nurse of pleasing contemplation
By the stream my wanderings lead.

It was not until the 1830s that the common man in America began to lose his bias against hunting and fishing. Henry W. Herbert, an English-man, writing under the pen name of Frank Forester, published essays and several books about hunting and fishing. Frank's influence as an outdoor writer has not since been matched. His writings inspired his readers to the point of action as attitudes changed. Rules of fair play and gentlemanly behavior in outdoor sports were emphasized. Through

Forester's efforts, American outdoorsmen began to be regarded as respectable citizens rather than irresponsible rowdies.

As the enjoyment of outdoor recreation became more acceptable, farsighted individuals saw the need for areas to be set aside where the common man could enjoy hunting, fishing, hiking, boating, nature study, and sightseeing. The first real step towards the establishment of such areas took place in 1831 with the establishment of a scenic cemetery at Mount Auburn, Massachusetts. The idea caught on and spread quickly. Cities soon began to plan for other open spaces for growing populations.

Thoreau's Walden took the enjoyment of the outdoors to a new height. His living example at Walden Pond captivated readers. Thoreau emitted a genuine inspiration through his unfailing perception. He clearly demonstrated the wisdom of finding God in nature, which helped to bring into the fold many who had previously considered "pursuits of nature" a waste of time and immoral. Thoreau revealed the benefits of and the importance of understanding every bit of God's Creation.

As attitudes towards the outdoors and recreational pursuits changed, people wanted more. Nature writers blossomed. A National Park System and a US Forest Service were created. The conservation movement grew. A Wildlife Refuge system was created and state game and fish agencies began improving opportunities for outdoorsmen. Most of the efforts that have improved fish and game habitats came about through the excise taxes paid on sporting goods and license fees - by hunters and fishermen.

With ninety-seven percent of our population living on three percent of the land, it is no wonder that participation in the hunting and fishing sports has been declining. Generations have been separated from the soil. Our nation has changed from a rural society to an urban society just since the 1930s, only 70 years!

Our conservation efforts today are dependent upon the support of the urban hunter and fisherman. Our efforts must focus on acquiring more wild lands near the urban areas so that the common man can continue to enjoy the outdoors on a regular basis. It is essential if our citizenry is going to continue participating in the healthy, wholesome, inspirational outdoor sports.

May the campfires continue to glow, the stews to simmer and the stories to flow freely.

Bill Cooper

DEDICATION

Kids are the future of the outdoor world. I dedicate this book to them. I love them—mine (Jenny, Jessica, Jayson, Jared, Carl and Cody), and all the kids like them. I have had the pleasure to share life with three kids born to me and three which I adopted. Jared, my last child born to me, was one of the unfortunates allergic to modern vaccines. Jared was left brain damaged at the tender age of four months. Yet, we splashed in the summer creeks, rolled in the autumn leaves, tossed snowballs, and smelled the spring wildflowers. During the 1991 turkey season, Jared slipped quietly into eternity fifteen days before his eleventh birthday. Jared taught me much about life and about the joys of being a kid. We will play together again someday.

I salute the thousands of kids across the country who enjoy the outdoors. The outdoors will provide untold hours of fun, relaxation, and escape from a hectic world. Go as often as you can to that "hiding place" which is special to you. Sit quietly. Think. Nap. Come away inspired and refreshed.

I dedicate this book especially to the JAKES (Juniors Acquiring Knowledge, Ethics & Sportsmanship) and the thousands of volunteers that lead them. JAKES is the youth organization of the National Wild Turkey Federation. Jared was a JAKE, too!

Bill Cooper

TABLE OF CONTENTS

Outdoor Celebrities

"Outdoor cookery has brought fame and fortune to many authors. It has brought me excess stomach acid and withering of the taste buds. The world of outdoor cookery is a grim, inhospitable one, strewn with pitfalls that would bring Julia Child to her knees."

Joel Vance, "Confessions of the Outdoor Maladroit"

OUTDOOR GRUB

It has long been a well known fact that in order to get the most from a trip into the outdoors, one must eat well. The hot dog and Twinkie meals of many modern day outdoorsmen leaves them coming up short in the stamina department. Therefore, food for the outdoors must be nutritious yet compact enough to be easily transported. The grub list, thus, becomes an important tool for the planning of any outdoor excursion. Compare yours with grub lists of other great outdoorsmen from the past.

Thoreau - 1846 "Keep it simple" was the philosophy by which Thoreau lived, even when trekking through the Maine woods. His grub list for a twelve-day trip with a companion and one Indian included the following: 28 pounds of ship's bread, 16 pounds of salt pork, 12 pounds of sugar, 3 pounds of coffee, 3 pounds of rice, 1 quart of Indian meal, 1 pint of salt, and 6 lemons. Simple!

The plan was to consume ¾ pound of bread and ½ pound of pork a day. Bland, no doubt. However, four cups of strong coffee each day, embellished with five teaspoons of sugar each, was sure to fire the coals!

Fresh fish and wild berries added zing to the menu, as did fried moose meat and summer duck.

While a guest at another's camp, it is said that Thoreau wolfed down "hot wheaten cakes...ham, eggs, potatoes, milk and cheese...and also some shad and salmon, tea sweetened with molasses, and sweet cakes...with cranberries for dessert." Outdoor appetites commonly foils simplicity!

Hemingway - 1919 Hemingway headed for the North Woods after his stint in World War I with the Italian army. He soloed the Fox River for trout. His menu appeared in the story "Big Two-Hearted River."

Hemingway liked cans. One meal consisted of canned pork and beans simmered with canned spaghetti. A whole bottle of ketchup topped the skillet. He lapped the concoction up with a loaf of bread.

Buckwheat flapjacks cooked in lard and covered with apple butter served as breakfast. Coffee stained with condensed milk washed the meal down. Leftover cakes were wrapped in paper and stuffed in a pocket for snacks. Raw onion sandwiches, dipped in cold stream water, made a lunch. Dinner, however, had to be three nice-sized trout!

L.L. Bean - 1942 Bean had a hearty appetite. His grub list for two men for six days made others look slight. Eleven pounds of bread, flour, cornmeal, oatmeal, pancake mix, cookies, doughnuts, 8 pounds of potatoes, 7 pounds of salt pork, bacon and beef, 7 pounds of canned goods, a dozen eggs, 2 pounds of sugar, 1¼ pounds of coffee and tea, 1 pound of syrup, ½ pound of salt and baking soda, plus pepper, vinegar, and mustard. All the food on the list weighed almost 40 pounds!

1970s - Thousands of canoers and backpackers had discovered freeze-dried foods. The variety was endless: freeze-dried eggs, beef stroganoff, turkey Tetrazzini, shrimp Alfredo, rice and chicken, pasta primavera, fruit crisps, and ice cream.

Freeze-dried foods were a disaster for many outdoorsmen. Hearty eaters had a tough time adjusting to the feather-light easy to prepare meals that tasted like cardboard.

Many outdoor cooks returned to the basic grub list , taking along what they liked most.

Bill Cooper - 1998 In my near half century on the planet I have sampled all the previously mentioned grub lists. As a child, pork and eggs and peanut butter sandwiches fired my excursions. Freeze-drieds made their way into my backpack decades later.

However, my outdoor counterparts and I prefer to eat well. A two-day float trip on the Big Piney River in the Missouri Ozarks required the following grub list for four: stir fry for dinner: 2 pounds of steak, 1 pound of carrots, 1 pound of cauliflower, 1 pound of broccoli, 1 large tomato, 1 small bottle of soy sauce, 6 large red apples with cinnamon and butter rolled in foil. Breakfast: 1 pound of bacon, 1 dozen eggs, 4 potatoes, 6 packets of oatmeal (which no one ate), 1 quart orange juice. Lunches: 1 pound bologna, 1 pound sliced roast beef, 1 tomato, 1 red onion, 1 small bottle mustard, ½ pound cheese. Snacks: 1 dozen fruit bars, 6 nectarines, 6 individual packets of peanut butter and crackers. Other items: 1 quart pink grapefruit juice, 4 quarts water frozen in quart containers, 6 coffee packets, 6 cup-of-soup packets, 1 35mm film canister each of salt, pepper, sugar, 1 three-ounce bottle of honey, 1 large bottle of white wine.

Our party of four was joined by eight other outdoor writers. The week-end excursion turned into a gravel bar culinary feast that would have been the envy of Thoreau and Hemingway. The eye appeal of green onions, bell peppers, banana peppers and seasoned chicken breasts slowly cooking over a campfire mesmerized our party. Wrapped in heated tortilla shells and doused with guacamole and hot sauce, the end product was nothing short of heavenly! Strawberries Romanoff served in long-stemmed wine glasses created a gravel bar atmosphere like few Ozark streams have witnessed. I love you, Hank Reifeiss!!

Bill Cooper

Big Game

7:15 AM   NOV 15

†David Besenger©19

THE GIFT

THE GIFT

It takes a hunter a second or two to straighten his or her thoughts when a 25-year dream suddenly materializes in front of them. Brad Harris will be the first to admit his mind was spinning when he saw a huge 16-point whitetail charging hard through the hardwoods toward his treestand.

"My first thoughts were, 'It's him, a Boone & Crockett buck,'" said Harris, a well-known whitetail expert/hunter and head of Lohman Game Calls' prestigious pro staff. "Even though it was running hard after a doe I could tell it was an awesome buck. The kind I've worked my tail off trying to get a shot at all my life!" But unlike the scenario that had replayed thousands of times in his mind, Harris didn't ready his rifle and mentally prepare himself for the shot when the buck burst onto the scene.

In any given year, Harris is afield chasing whitetails close to 100 days a season. He'll actually begin with scouting when the previous season ends, walking his hunting grounds looking for any rubs, scrapes or bedding areas that could shed some light on what to expect in the upcoming fall. Late summer, he'll be glassing hay and soybean fields at dusk, looking for bachelor groups of whitetails. He'll be in treestands when the first seasons open in the north until the final seasons close in the south.

Most of the hunts are "business" related; that is, either shooting video for Lohman, Realtree Outdoors or guiding. But there is one long weekend in the midst of it all when you won't find Harris "working" in the trophy whitetail woods - even though mid-November could be prime time for Harris to take that 160-plus B & C buck he's always dreamed of in Iowa, Illinois or Kansas. Instead, he'll be in his native Missouri Ozarks following a long weekend tradition that means more to him than all of the other hunts combined.

"We've been doing a family deer camp for as long as I can remember," said Harris. "I have four brothers, plus some uncles, brothers-in-law and some good friends that have been hunting together for years. To me, it's the most important hunt of the year for several reasons. One is that it's for relaxation. I may take the video camera, but it's not the most important thing. Mainly, though, it's because it's with my family. They're by far the most important thing a person can have, and to get to share the outdoors, something I also dearly love, with them - it's tough to put into words."

Those last few annual hunts have been especially dear to Harris because "family" hasn't just meant his brothers. Up until he was drawn away by the pressures and tight schedule of college, Brad Jr., Harris' oldest son, was his favorite hunting partner at deer camp. For the past three seasons his youngest son, 13-year-old Brent, has been his main sidekick.

The Harris clan hunts a huge farm of stereotypical hardwood ridges in central Missouri. Though not an area known for huge bucks, it has plenty of whitetails and is big enough to hold their traditional tent-style camp and a dozen or so hunters. As usual, the crew gathered the day before the season opener. Late that afternoon father and son eased along a ridge to check a favored hotspot.

"It's up near a saddle on a hardwood ridge, on an edge where brush meets open hardwoods," said Harris. "It's a natural travel route for whitetails. We've hunted it for three or four years and it's always been good. It's about a mile back in there, so there's no human disturbance and no real need to get in and scout it out. We just slip in the afternoon before the season opens and check the sign."

That afternoon, they found the best sign—fresh tracks, huge rubs and scrapes—to be downwind of the stand. Together they quietly moved the Trax, "Me and My Buddy" ladder stand, 150 yards to work the wind and headed back to camp. That night brought the welcome opening-eve feast, renewal of old friendships and the reliving of past hunts and camps. It also brought a less than desirable weather system.

"You always go to bed dreaming about a cold and calm morning, but we had neither," said Harris. "When we woke up, the wind was blowing about 30 mph and the temperature was downright warm. It was less than ideal."

As he had during the previous two seasons, Harris went along with Brent, as much to instruct as to assist. Big bucks, both admit, were the furthest thing from their mind. The boy had taken a dandy 130-class, 10-pointer his first season, and everyone in camp had teased it was probably all downhill from there. By the end of that fateful day, November 15, they would all learn that they had been wrong.

Harris and Brent climbed into the stand well before daylight, the elder holding a video camera and the younger his Remington Model 7 Youth Rifle in .243. Things didn't look good as daylight broke.

"The main thing was the wind," recalled Harris. "I can still remember waves of leaves just blowing by our stand. And that was at ground-level; the treetops were really whipping. I knew that deer don't like to move as well in the wind and we couldn't hear a darned thing but that wind."

Not long after sunrise, Harris turned and saw a nice eight-point buck working about 60 yards behind the stand. "He was chasing a doe, which you know is always loud on dry leaves, and I hadn't even heard him," said Harris. "I tried to get Brent turned around in time for a shot but the buck didn't stick around long enough. I leaned forward and told Brent we were really going to have to pay attention. He would be on his own watching in front of the stand while I watched behind."

Less than an hour later, Harris caught sight of Brent slowly sliding his rifle into position. Following where the gun was pointing, Harris caught sight of a doe running hard. Not far behind her, and moving just as fast was the kind of whitetail Harris had always dreamed about.

"I'll admit that one of my first thoughts was that it just wasn't fair," recalls Harris, with a chuckle. "Here was the buck of my lifetime and I look down and see it's a little boy holding the gun. But then I realized what little boy that was."

Harris' first concern was to find some way to stop the streaking buck for the 13-year-old who had no experience at hitting moving deer. As luck would have it, Harris had a prototype of Lohman's new Monster Buck Grunt call, a grunt tube with a megaphone that's made for when volume is needed.

"It's just by the grace of God that I had it, the only one, with me and had the presence of mind to use it," said Harris. "It's made to be loud and it wouldn't have worked if it was any quieter. I hit it once and the buck never paused. I blew it again and he stopped, perfectly broadside at just 24 yards."

Harris was just getting the huge whitetail focused in the video camera when Brent shot and the buck bolted, passing within eight yards of the stand. To Harris' surprise, the buck stopped abruptly 35 yards behind their tree. "I was about to panic," he recalls. "The buck sure showed no sign of being hit. I couldn't hardly believe we'd even had a chance at a buck like that, and then he stops and gives Brent another shot."

Harris quietly tried to whisper encouragement and instruction to his son as the boy tried to bolt a fresh round into the chamber and swivel around for a second shot. "I was trying to stay calm," recalls Harris. "I was saying 'take your time, squeeze the trigger' to Brent but inwardly I was thinking, 'My gosh, hurry up, he's not going to stand there all day.'" The boy eventually tried a shot which Harris knew was most certainly a clean miss.

It's still like the whole thing is frozen in time," recalls Harris. "I was just kind of numbed by the whole thing. I looked down at Brent and he just matter-of-factly said, 'that sure was a big one, wasn't it, Dad.' I told him I doubted he'd ever know just how big that buck was and that it would probably be the biggest he'd ever see in the wild. I was heartbroken but I didn't want to make Brent feel bad because he'd missed."

To both teach his son some valuable lessons and rule out any possibility of a hit, Harris and Brent slowly worked over everything that had happened. "Where were you holding on the first shot?" Harris asked.

"I was holding right behind the shoulder," was the boy's calm answer.

"So, do you think you might have hit him?" asked Harris.

"Dad," answered Brent, "I know I hit him with that first shot!"

"I didn't know what to make of that because I was thinking hard that he had missed because of the way the buck acted," said Harris. "But he had such confidence. I asked him about the second shot and he admitted that he'd rushed it and missed, which I knew that he had."

After waiting several more minutes, they descended their stand and started looking for signs of a hit where the buck had passed next to the stand. Within a minute or two Harris found a pea-sized speck of red on a leaf. He then followed the trail to where the buck had stood for several seconds before Brent's second shot. To their disappointment, they found no blood.

"A lot of things were going through my mind," said Harris. "I wondered if the buck had maybe been injured earlier in a fight or maybe had cut itself slightly on a fence or stob. We moved 30 yards down the trail, to where we'd last seen the buck and weren't finding anything. It was looking pretty bleak when Brent, in his same calm manner, said, 'Dad, here's more.' It wasn't much but it got our hopes up."

Harris found himself facing what he knew could be some important decisions. Many who've met the man, rate him as the best in the nation at reading sign and recovering deer. He didn't like what he was seeing or the options he was having to face.

"I could tell by the color of the blood that the buck might go a ways before going down," said Harris. "Most times I just get the heck out and give the deer several hours, like maybe comeback late that afternoon. But I looked at the forest floor and saw all those leaves being blown about and I began to wonder if there would be any trail left within a few minutes, let alone later that day."

He calmly explained the entire scenario to Brent, suggesting that they had no other choice but to take up the trail and hope for the best. Harris assured his son that the buck might be jumped and suggested that it might be best if he carried the rifle instead of the inexperienced shooter. Brent quickly handed over the gun, insisting that he wanted to do what was best to get the buck humanely down as soon as possible.

Hunched over and straining their eyes, the two hunters moved slowly along the buck's trail, finding the occasional sign on a leaf that the wind hadn't blown away. They were so intent on their search for sign that they walked right up on the deer. "He got up just about 15 yards away," said Harris. "You could tell that he wasn't doing too good. He was just standing there. I raised the gun, put the scope on the buck and was about to shoot when I thought, 'This isn't right, it's his buck. He should put him down.' Then as I was handing the rifle to Brent the buck ran off."

Harris still shivers when he recalls the emotions that swept through his body. "If I'd have just left Brent to carry the rifle or made the shot myself it would have been over easily right there," he said. "As it was, I was left literally feeling sick and wondering what to do next. The buck was up and moving toward the neighboring property where another hunter might get it. Worse yet, I knew once up, it might run off and hide in some thicket and never be found."

The veteran hunter then paused to gather his thoughts, and told his eager son that the buck now knew that it was being followed. No doubt it was stopped again on some ridge, watching it's back trail, and that one more encounter could push it out of their lives forever. Blowing leaves and disappearing trail or not, they had no choice but to back off and come back that afternoon.

During those long midday hours, Harris explained to Brent the strategy they would follow. Hopefully they could pick up enough scattered sign to follow the buck. If not, they'd follow the trail it was using. Should they not find it before dark, he assured his son the entire camp would gladly sacrifice some hunting time the next day to thoroughly scour the surrounding woods.

But luckily there was still plenty of sign to follow and the buck was found not 100 yards from where it had last been seen.

"I looked up and saw it and let Brent go on up to it first," said Harris. "I wanted him to experience it for a while by himself before I got up and started getting excited. The buck was laying so that all we could see was the side with the five typical points on it, which was darned impressive. When Brent lifted it, the other side, the one with 11 points, came up. I'll never forget the look on his face or how excited I felt."

Brent's deer grossed an impressive 192⅜ Boone & Crockett points, which is especially awesome since one side is perfectly typical. In fact, had the typical side had a match, it easily would have made that B & C category. Had the non-typical side had a match, it would have made the grade as non-typical, too. Most agree that the unique father-son story behind the buck makes it one of the most memorable bucks of last season, record book or not.

Harris is quick to say that he wouldn't change a thing about it—not the score, not the hunt and most importantly, not who got the buck. "You know, I've had a lot of people say that it's a shame that I didn't get the buck instead of Brent," said Harris. "But I've gotten to where I almost laugh out loud at that. I'm much, much more excited because my son got it. I could get a Boone & Crockett with my bow next fall and it honestly wouldn't mean as much to me. Next to my family, the time we spent getting that buck is the thrill of my life, and I know it's going to be the thrill of his life...and we got to share it together."

—Michael Pearce

"The Gift," written by outdoor writer Michael Pearce has been reprinted courtesy of Harris Publications' Outdoor Magazine Group. The original story ran in *Whitetail Hunting Strategies* November 1997. Back orders and subscriptions can be obtained by calling 1-888-345-BUCK.

DOC DETTMER'S
BACON WRAPPED VENISON
Submitted by: Scott Bennett

This recipe was given to me by my dear friend and NWTF National Board Member, Dr. Robert (WRGE) Dettmer. It is guaranteed to change the way you look at venison!

6 ounces venison fillets	Hickory smoked bacon
Garlic salt	Freeze-dried coffee
Toothpicks	Mortar and pestle
Hickory chips	Grill (charcoal or gas)

Cut of venison needed: backstrap or part of rump roast.

Cut meat so that you can butterfly and make into 6 ounce fillets. Once butterflied, wrap hickory smoked bacon around each fillet and keep in place with toothpicks. Sprinkle garlic salt generously over both sides of fillet and let sit 5 minutes. Pour freeze-dried coffee into mortar (bowl and large spoon can be used) and pulverize crystals into powder. Sprinkle powder on both sides of fillets and let sit 10 minutes or until coffee looks like it has melted. Once grill is ready, place fillets on grill and cover. Grill on each side exactly 6 minutes for medium rare.

NOTE: To enjoy this recipe to the fullest, it is important not to cook venison too long as to dry out the meat. Prepared right, this will be some of the best venison you have ever experienced.

Grill Preparation
Make sure fire is medium hot to hot before you place meat on grill. For best results, soak hickory chips in water 2 hours before ready to cook venison. Drain excess water from hickory chips and pour chips over coals prior to grilling venison.

BAR-B-QUE BLACK BEAR BACK STRAPS
Submitted by: Greg Nixon

Black bear back straps   **Ground pepper**
Jalapeño peppers   **Favorite bar-b-que sauce**

Cut one full back strap into quarters. Marinate overnight in covered dish in refrigerator, adding 1 cup jalapeño juice with ½ cup jalapeño peppers and two tablespoons ground pepper. Place on grill, rotating every 5 minutes, for about 20 minutes.

QUICK BEAN SOUP
Submitted by: Denny Brauer

1½	pounds deer or elk burger	1-2	cans tomatoes and chilies
1	onion, chopped	2	(15 ounce) cans of ranch style beans
3	(10 ounce) cans minestrone soup		

Brown meat with onions and drain. Combine with other ingredients and simmer for 1 hour.

BLACK BEAR BRATS
Submitted by: Greg Nixon

Ground bear meat   **Jalapeño seasoning**
Ground pork shoulders

Mix 1 pound of ground pork for every 4 pounds of ground black bear. Combine and mix thoroughly. Add 1 tablespoon of ground jalapeño seasoning per pound. Stuff in casings and freeze. Cook on grill, broil or bake for the best brats ever.

BLACK BEAR CHILI

Submitted by: Greg Nixon

1-1½	pounds ground bear meat or chunk bear meat	2	bell peppers
1	quart tomato juice	1	large can chili beans
2	large onions		Chili powder

Brown 1 to 1½ pounds of ground bear meat or chunk bear meat in skillet and drain. Place in pot. Add one quart tomato juice, diced onions, diced bell peppers, 2 tablespoons chili powder, can of chili beans. Add water if desired; simmer for 2-3 hours.

BEAR STEAKS OR CHOPS

Submitted by: Greg Nixon

Bear steaks of chops	Lemon juice salt
Marinade	Black pepper

Cut steaks or chops from rump and remove excess fat. Marinate for 24 hours in water mixed with 2 cups lemon juice, 4 tablespoons salt, and 1 tablespoon black pepper. Grill on hot charcoal fire or in oven broiler.

MOOSE STEAKS

Submitted by: Jerry Martin

Cut steaks ½-inch to ⅝-inch thick.

Marinate in milk for 2 hours. Roll in flour, salt and pepper and fry. Make milk gravy from drippings.

VENISON STEAK À LA CALVADOS

Submitted by: Kate Fiduccia

4	1-inch thick loin fillets		Thyme, to taste
¼	cup butter, clarified		Coriander, to taste
¼	cup Calvados (apple brandy)		Sweet marjoram, to taste
			Black pepper, to taste
1	cup heavy cream		Summer savory, to taste
½	pound venison bits	1	pulverized bay leaf
3	strips bacon, uncooked	⅓	cup bread crumbs
½	cup corn	1	beaten egg

This recipe I prepare in two steps, with the meat being prepared first. Take bits of venison and bacon and either chop them very fine or place them in a small food processor and mix on high for 10 seconds, at the most. Mix in the corn and six spices by hand or with a spoon. Once well blended, mix in the bread crumbs and beaten egg. Shape into patties and cook them starting in a cold, ungreased pan. If the corn "pops" while it is cooking, partially cover the pan with a lid. Remove from heat when cooked thoroughly. Keep warm on a heated platter.

Season the venison fillets with ground peppercorns (plain pepper will do, too). Heat the clarified butter over medium/high heat (don't let it burn), then sauté the fillets in the butter letting the side you sauté first, sear well, for about two minutes. Turn over and sauté the other side. Just before it is done, carefully add the brandy, and light it. The flames will die out as the alcohol burns. Once the flame has died, remove the fillets from the pan, reduce the temperature to low and add the cream. Stir well and season with salt and pepper. Let it simmer for about five minutes.

At this point, I like to serve the creamy sauce in a separate side dish because the venison fillet and the sausage have a unique flavor of their own. The cream sauce adds another different dimension. Enjoy.

CALZONE

Submitted by: Jim Casada

¾-1	pound ground venison	¼	teaspoon oregano
½	cup chopped onion	1	14-ounce jar tomato and
½	cup sliced fresh		basil spaghetti sauce
	mushrooms	1	(8-ounce) package refrig-
1	clove garlic, minced		erator crescent rolls
¼	cup venison kielbasa		Flour
¼	teaspoon Italian	8-10	ounces grated mozzarella
	seasoning		cheese

Sauté venison, onion, garlic, and mushrooms until vegetables are tender and venison is browned. Add venison kielbasa and ¼ teaspoon Italian seasoning. Simmer to heat kielbasa.

Place two triangles of crescent dough together to form a rectangle and press edges together to seal. Roll lightly in flour. In center of rectangle place two tablespoons venison and vegetable mixture. Top with two tablespoons spaghetti sauce and grated cheese. Fold one edge of dough over and seal edges together. Repeat procedure. Place in ovenproof dish. Pour remaining sauce over each. If any venison remains, sprinkle it on top of sauce. Top with cheese.

Bake at 350 degrees for twenty minutes.

Four servings.

> *"A hunter's skills must go well beyond merely sighting and cleanly killing his game. He must be able to identify its habitat through knowledge of the appropriate vegetation and terrain. He must be woodsman enough to recognize the signs of game presence before he sees the game itself. He looks for the things his game will feed upon and the thing that will feed upon his game. He knows how game species are effected by the activities of their non-game neighbors."*
>
> —Charles F. Waterman

NO PEEK DEER CASSEROLE

Submitted by: Kevin Howard

The following recipe is a favorite at the home of Kevin on busy days. Since it is cooked in a slow cooker, the dish can be prepared in the morning before going to work and its enticing smells welcome you home for supper.

2	pounds deer loin, cut into 1-inch pieces	1	4-ounce can whole mushrooms
1	envelope onion soup mix	½	cup water or red wine
1	10½-ounce can of cream of mushroom soup		

Combine all ingredients in slow cooker. Stir together well. Cover and cook on low for 8 to 12 hours. Serve over noodles or rice. (High: 4 to 5 hours). This recipe may be doubled.

VENISON STEAK AU POIVRE

Submitted by: Peter Fiduccia

8	loin steaks, ½-inch thick, lightly pounded	8	ounces espagnole or brown sauce
2	ounces clarified butter	4	shakes Worcestershire
1½	ounces brandy	4	tablespoons whole black pepper, crushed
1½-2	tablespoons Dijon mustard		
4	ounces heavy cream	2	tablespoons shallots

In a sauté pan heat clarified butter. Coat steak lightly with crushed black pepper and place in pan. Brown meat nicely and turn. Add shallots. Remove pan from stove, add brandy. Be careful when returning pan to flame (the alcohol will ignite and possibly explode if your pan is too hot!) Remove meat and keep warm. To the pan add Dijon mustard, Worcestershire and espagnole, bring to a simmer. Add heavy cream; again bring to a simmer. Add meat and heat through. Serve.

NOTE: The doneness of the meat desired should be reached before adding the brandy. Due to the time involved in preparing brown sauce, I suggest using a convenience product.

DEER KABOBS
Submitted by: Woo Daves

Cut hind quarter or loin into bite size chunks (3 pounds or so). Combine McCormick's Meat Marinade with ½ cup of oil, 2 tablespoons of vinegar, and a can of beer. Marinate the meat for 8 hours in McCormick's Meat Marinade. (It must be McCormick's.) Then wrap a piece of beef bacon around deer kabobs and put on skewers. Cook on grill till the bacon is done, rotate the skewers while cooking. The deer will be ready when the bacon is done, so do not overcook! Delicious and mouth watering!

VENISON CHILI
Submitted by: Karen Mehall

1-1½	pounds venison	3	cans (14½ ounce) kidney beans, undrained
½	pound sliced fresh mushrooms	½	teaspoon hot sauce
1	green pepper, coarsely chopped	½	teaspoon cayenne pepper
1	can (14½ ounce) sliced, stewed tomatoes	1	teaspoon cumin
		2-3	dashes black pepper
1	can (6 ounce) tomato paste	2-3	dashes crushed red pepper
		2-3	dashes garlic powder

Combine ingredients in a four quart crock pot (slow cooker). Cook on low for about eight hours and serve.

Optional: Top with chopped onion and shredded cheddar cheese.

VENISON JERKY

Submitted by: Karen Mehall

3½-4	pounds venison	2	teaspoons smoke flavoring
2	cups apple juice	2	teaspoons black pepper
5	ounces Teriyaki sauce	1	teaspoon steak sauce
5	ounces soy sauce		

Slice venison into ⅛-inch strips and marinade overnight.

Dehydrator method: Place strips in dehydrator for 8 to 12 hours. (Note: If your dehydrator has a fan, the time will be less.) Jerky is done when all moisture is out. Store in an air tight container.

Oven Method: Line bottom of oven with foil and place oven rack as high as possible. Put oven temperature on lowest setting. Hang venison strips from oven rack with toothpicks and let them dry for about 6 hours with the oven door cracked open until moisture is out. Be careful that the strips do not become crunchy. Store in an air tight container.

"Although his time in the woods may be limited, the most successful sportsman takes great advantage of the privilege of hunting— a privilege that becomes more and more valuable as game fields shrink and wildlife competes at an increasing disadvantage with the expanding environment of mankind. The hunter's bag and shooting person are limited by law, but if he knows his hunting grounds he hunts better and enjoys it more. He may find more game and kill less of it."

—Charles F. Waterman

DEER BURGER MEATLOAF

Submitted by: Tony Allbright

2	pounds deer burger, ground	¼	teaspoon each dry mustard, sage, celery salt, garlic
1	cup dry bread crumbs		
1¼	cup milk		Salt
1	egg, beaten	1	tablespoon Worcestershire sauce
¼	cup onion, minced		
1¼	teaspoon salt		

Heat oven to 350 degrees. Mix all ingredients; shape into loaf, put in shallow pan, spread catsup on top. Bake 1½ hours.

DEER LIVER PÂTÉ

Submitted by: Bob McNally

In many deer camps, venison liver is not saved, and a hunter who keeps track of such things can gather several before the end of the season.

With 3 to 6 whole livers in hand, smoke them on a simple, easy-to-use water smoker (made by Brinkman, and others). Hickory nuts work well, but so does wood of apple, cherry, etc.

Next, cut the smoked livers into chunks, and grind in a food processor, grinder or even a blender. To about 1 pound of ground, smoked venison liver, add ½ cup mustard. Play with the ingredients to get the right consistency. Mix, then process again until it becomes a pâté or meat spread. Serve on crackers and eat as a before-dinner snack. It's sensational. It can be made in large quantities and frozen in cottage cheese type containers.

DEER CHILI

Submitted by: Chad Brauer

1½	pounds deer burger	1	package chili seasoning
1	can kidney beans	2	tablespoons chili powder
2	cans chili beans	1	teaspoon hot sauce
1	can tomatoes, chopped	¼	cup brown sugar
1	(64 ounce) can tomato juice		

Brown deer burger in Dutch oven; drain fat. Add next 8 ingredients. Bring to a boil; reduce heat; simmer over low heat for 30 minutes. Serve with chopped onions, shredded cheese, and sour cream.

DEER BURGER CHILI

Submitted by: Tony Allbright

1	large onion	1½	pounds deer burger
1	clove garlic		

Brown above ingredients together and drain off grease. Add: 1 can V-8 Juice, 1 cup coffee, good pinch of red pepper, ½ teaspoon cumin, 1 bay leaf, 1½ tablespoon chili powder, small pinch basil, 2 teaspoons salt, 1 tablespoon sugar. Simmer for one hour; add 22-ounce can chili beans. Simmer ½ hour.

DEER STRIPS

Submitted by: Brian Jenkins

1	pound deer meat		Table salt
4	tablespoons cooking oil	1-2	onions
	Garlic salt	⅓	cup water

Take deer meat and cut into ⅜-inch strips. Sprinkle meat with garlic salt, pepper and table salt to taste, place in skillet with hot cooking oil and brown well on both sides. Add water and onions; cover and simmer until desired tenderness.

TENDER DEER ROAST
Submitted by: Brenda Valentine

Any lesser cut of venison, such as the neck roast or front shoulder can be made scrumptious with this recipe.

Put meat into crockpot or roasting pan; pour one can of lemon-lime soda over the meat; sprinkle one package of onion soup mix over the meat and into the soda. Cover tightly and slow cook until done.

This is one of my favorite dishes to put on early in the day and forget about. The flavorful meat is always fork tender. A very welcome supper when I've been out hunting all day.

ELK KABOBS ON THE GRILL
Submitted by: Steve Puppe

3-4	pounds of elk loin	1	large onion
1	large bottle Italian dressing	1	large can chunk pineapple
1	pound whole mushrooms		

Cut elk loin into 1½-inch chunks. Marinate in Italian dressing for at least 12 hours. Alternate ingredients on skewer. Grill over medium heat to desired tenderness. Do not overcook.

Serve over rice. This also works well with venison or moose.

ELK CAVATINI

Submitted by: Mark Drury

1	pound elk burger	½	pound fresh mushrooms
1	large onion, chopped		or 1 can of mushrooms
1	medium green pepper, sliced thin	1	(12-ounce) jar of your favorite spaghetti sauce
3	small zucchini, sliced and split in halves (about 1½ inches in diameter)		Parmesan cheese
		1	cup mozzarella cheese
		3	kinds of pasta, 4 ounces each

Cook meat, onion, pepper and zucchini in non-stick pan until no longer pink. Add mushrooms, cook until tender. Add spaghetti sauce, cooked pasta, 1 cup mozzarella cheese. Stir until mixed well. Serve immediately. Garnish with Parmesan cheese.

VENISON FORRESTIERE

Submitted by: Peter J. Fiduccia

6	venison steaks, 2½ to 3 ounces each	1	ounce brandy or 3 ounces red wine
¾	cup mushrooms, sliced		Chopped parsley
½	cup cooked bacon, roughly chopped	6	ounces espagnole
	Butter		Seasoned flour, as needed
		1	tablespoon shallots

Prepare venison for cooking. Heat butter in sauté pan. Dredge venison in seasoned flour, add to pan. Brown nicely and turn. Push venison to one side of pan. Add shallots, mushrooms, bacon and parsley. Deglaze with brandy or wine. Add espagnole. Simmer for 3 to 5 minutes.

Serves 3.

FRIED VENISON

Submitted by: Larry Weishuhn

Using loin or muscles separated out of the hindquarter, cut steaks across the grain, approximately ¾-inch thick. Dip in whole milk and then flour. In a cast iron skillet heat bacon drippings until extremely hot, so when you drop in a tiny bit of flour, the grease bubbles.

When grease is truly hot, gently drop in floured steaks, fry until juices start coming out of the "up" side of the steak, then turn and fry for about another 15 to 30 seconds, depending upon the size of the steaks. Remove from the frying pan and add other steaks, keeping them hot on top of the stove.

When all steaks have been fried, I generally plan on frying about 12 to 14 ounces of pre-fried steak per person, pour most of the grease out of the pan. Turn heat down. Add diced shallots (or onions if not available) and heat until they become soft, or onions slightly transparent. Then scatter a small handful of flour into the pan, allowing it to brown with the onions. Then add milk used to wet the steaks originally, all the while stirring. Add just enough milk while stirring so the gravy becomes "syrupy" in consistency. At this point pour into bowl.

Serve fried venison with mashed potatoes (to go along with the gravy), along with fried okra, and a tossed green salad. Allow diners to season with salt and pepper to their personal taste.

DEER TENDERLOIN

Submitted by: Walter Parrott

Slice deer tenderloin into ¾-inch steaks. Marinate in Dale's Sauce for 30 minutes. Wrap a strip of bacon around each tenderloin steak. Grill until done.

FIRST NIGHT VENISON ORIENTAL

Submitted by: Jim Low

1	pound of back strap, cut in slices	1	medium gingerroot, peeled and diced
			Juice of 1 lime
	Marinate one hour in:	4	large cloves of garlic, diced
4	ounces soy sauce		
4	ounces white cooking wine	1	teaspoon ground black pepper

Place meat and marinade in tight-sealing plastic container and freeze.

When packing for your backpacking trip, place the frozen meat container in a sealable plastic bag and place it deep inside your pack. It will be thawed by the end of the first day's hike.

At the end of the trail, cut two large green bell peppers and one large red bell pepper into ½-inch strips. Simmer the meat in the marinade until tender. Add pepper strips and cook briefly, leaving pepper slightly crunchy.

Serve over prepared instant rice. Enough to satisfy two hungry trekkers.

GREEN PEPPER ELK STEAK

Submitted by: Jim Strelec

1½	pounds steak	1	cup bouillon
2	onions, sliced	1	teaspoon Worcestershire sauce
1	teaspoon thyme		
1	teaspoon salt	3	tablespoons cooking oil
¼	teaspoon pepper	3	green peppers, cut in strips
½	cup red wine		

Cut meat into 4 steaks. Brown in hot fat in heavy skillet. Add onions, thyme, bouillon, salt and pepper. Cover and simmer 1 hour or until tender. Add green pepper, wine and Worcestershire sauce and simmer 20 minutes.

VENISON JERKY

Submitted by: Shirley Grenoble

Here is my absolute favorite jerky recipe given to me many years ago by John Olson of Galeton, Pennsylvania.

3	pounds venison	½	teaspoon black pepper
1	tablespoon salt	⅓	cup soy sauce
1	teaspoon onion powder	3	tablespoons liquid smoke
1	teaspoon garlic powder	¼	teaspoon saltpeter

Cut meat in small strips about the size of a cigarette. Remove all fat and gristle. Marinate overnight in above seasonings. Stir several times so meat becomes all the same color.

Drain meat. Pat dry with paper towels. Spread on cake cooling racks in a shallow pan. Put in oven. Dry in very low heat, turning several times until dry. Dry until stiff. Store in a dry place in a covered jar. Keeps indefinitely.

ROAST VENISON WITH MUSHROOMS

Submitted by: Larry Whiteley

4	pound venison rump roast	4	medium potatoes Salt and pepper
1	(10¾ ounce) can cream of mushroom soup		

Place the venison roast on a large piece of heavy-duty aluminum foil and put both of them in a roasting pan. Pour the can of soup over the top of the roast and sprinkle with a little salt and pepper. Close the foil around the roast securely and place the roasting pan in a preheated 350 degree oven. Roast for 1½ hours and remove from the oven. Open the foil and add 4 potatoes that have been scrubbed (not peeled) and cut in half. Seal the foil again, and return the pan to the oven for another hour of roasting.

To serve, thinly slice the venison roast and ladle the pieces with the mushroom sauce.

Serves 4.

MARISOL RANCH STEW
Submitted by: Larry Weishuhn

Cut venison, portions of hindquarter, into 1-inch square cubes, approximately 24 ounces. In a large stew pot, pour in sufficient bacon drippings to cover the bottom and heat. Add a teaspoon of ground chili pepper along with a couple dashes of garlic powder. When the grease is hot, drop in cubed venison, and sear all sides of the cubes in the bacon drippings.

Once all the cubes have been seared, reduce heat and pour in warm water so all the meat is covered, by at least 2 inches of water. Set on medium heat and cover with lid. Allow to cook for about 15 minutes, then check water level and add a 10½ to 12 ounce can of beef broth, and a 14 to 16 ounce can of peeled whole tomatoes. Also add two large white onions, which have been quartered. Then close the pot with the lid and allow to cook for another 15 minutes on medium heat.

While cooking, peel and cube 4 fairly large potatoes. Then place potatoes into the stew pot, stirring them into the mixture. Set on low heat and allow to cook for a minimum of 1 hour. In some instances it might take two hours on low heat. Check the stew periodically to be certain there is about 2 inches or more of fluid above the meat and potato mixture. If fluid level needs replenishing, add more water.

Approximately 30 minutes before meal time, put two tablespoons of flour in a water glass. Then add water, stirring all the while to make a thin "syrupy" mixture. Pour this mixture into the stew and stir to thicken it somewhat. Heat for a short while, and then serve, along with jalapeños and crackling corn bread. Guaranteed to take the chill out and have diners looking for more.

LOIN STEAK WITH CRAB AND SHRIMP SAUCE

Submitted by: Jim Casada

1   **pound loin steaks, cut**   1   **tablespoon margarine**
     ½-inch thick   **Salt and pepper to taste**
1   **tablespoon olive oil**

Heat olive oil and margarine in large skillet and quickly cook venison loin until medium-rare. Place on platter and keep warm. It is best to cook loin after sauce has started thickening.

Crab and Shrimp Sauce

2   **tablespoons olive oil**   ½   **pound surimi crabmeat**
½   **pound fresh mushrooms,**   **(or real crab)**
     sliced   12   **medium shrimp, cooked**
2   **cups whipping cream**   **and shelled**
¼   **cup White Zinfandel wine**
¼   **cup margarine, cut into**
     12 pieces

Heat two tablespoons oil in large skillet. Add mushrooms to skillet and sauté five minutes. Add cream and wine and reduce until thickened (about 10 to 12 minutes). Season with salt and pepper. Stir in margarine one piece at a time incorporating each piece completely before adding next. Add crabmeat and shrimp and heat through, about one minute. Pour over venison. Serve immediately.

Four servings.

"Simplicity in all things is the secret of the wilderness and one of its most valuable lessons. It is what we leave behind that is important. I think the matter of simplicity goes further than just food, equipment, and unnecessary gadgets; it goes into the matter of thoughts and objectives as well. When in the wilds, we must not carry our problems with us or the joy is lost."

—Sigurd Olson

VENISON MEATY CORNBREAD

Submitted by: Brad Harris

3	tablespoons butter or margarine	1	(15 ounce can) tomato sauce
1	cup onions, diced	3	tablespoons chili powder
1	cup green peppers, chopped	2	teaspoons salt
2	pounds ground venison	½	teaspoon pepper

Brown onions, pepper and meat in butter. Add seasonings and tomato sauce. Simmer 15 minutes, then place in a 9x13 inch baking dish. Top with cornbread mixture below.

Topping

2	cups yellow cornmeal	1	teaspoon baking powder
½	teaspoon baking soda	1	teaspoon salt
2	beaten eggs	6	tablespoons melted butter
1	cup plain yogurt		
¼	cup water		

Add liquids to dry ingredients; stir until moistened. Spread over meat mixture and bake at 425 degrees for 25 minutes.

BIG GAME LOAF

Submitted by: Mark Drury

1	pound big game burger	1	tablespoon Worcestershire sauce
1	medium tomato, chopped		
2	eggs	1	can mushrooms
1	medium onion, chopped		Salt and pepper to taste
¾	cup crushed crackers		Catsup
1	tablespoon soy sauce		

Preheat oven to 350 degrees. Combine and mix well all ingredients except catsup. Grease a loaf pan, put meat mixture in pan evenly. Cover top with catsup. Bake at 350 degrees for 1 hour and 45 minutes.

Serves 4.

NOTE: Chopped bacon can be added for flavor.

VENISON MEDALLIONS WITH A BLACK AND RED PEPPERCORN SAUCE

Submitted by: Kate Fiduccia

6¾-inch thick medallions from the venison loin
Salt, to taste
½ cup clarified butter
3 tablespoons Applejack brandy
1 large shallot, minced
1 teaspoon black and red peppercorns, coarsely crushed
2 cups beef bouillon (slightly thickened with a brown roux or corn starch)
1 cup heavy cream

Sprinkle the salt over both sides of the medallions. Sauté them over medium high heat in 4 tablespoons of clarified butter until golden brown on both sides. Pour off the butter, turn the heat a little lower and add the Applejack. (For those who have it available, use Calvados. It has a stronger apple taste to it.) Heat the brandy and then ignite it with a match. When the flames die out, remove the medallions from the pan to a warm dish.

Add the remaining clarified butter to the pan and add the minced shallot and crushed peppercorns. Sauté until the shallots are translucent (do not brown) and then add the beef bouillon. Stir occasionally and keep the sauce at a simmer until it is reduced by half. Pour in the cream (make sure it is at room temperature), stir and keep it at a low simmer until it reaches your desired consistency.

Place the medallions back in the pan just to re-warm them. Serve with Au Gratin or new potatoes with onions and roasted peppers.

Some of the happiest hunting is hopeless. The mule deer hunter turns away from the big buck's toe-dragged print in fresh snow and traces the route of a cougar, knowing from long experience that he will sight the cat only by coincidence and that before the day ends, the cougar probably will be trailing him."

—Charles F. Waterman

STUFFED DEER PEPPERS

Submitted by: Steve Stoltz

1	pound ground venison	1	(14.5 ounce) can of diced
1	egg		tomatoes
½	cup rice (any brand)	1	(6 ounce) can of tomato
1	medium yellow onion		paste
4	medium size bell peppers		

First cut around the stem and "gut" your green peppers. Then dice yellow onion. Mix rice, onion, and egg with ground venison. Stuff meat mixture into each pepper and place peppers in medium size sauce pan (for stove top) or a medium size baking dish. (I prefer a "Dutch" oven with lid). Next mix tomato paste with 1½ cups of water and then add diced tomatoes. Pour tomato mixture over peppers, cover with lid and let simmer on stove top for approximately 1½ hours. Or if baking, pre-heat oven to 340 degrees. Cover with lid and bake peppers at 340 degrees for approximately 2½ hours. Cooking time varies with size of peppers. Salt and pepper to taste.

When serving, I suggest cutting stuffed pepper up on the plate and pour tomato sauce from the pot over the meat and pepper.

Serve with fresh baked cornbread and fresh green onions. What a meal!

HOBO DISH

Submitted by: Bill Cooper

1	pound ground deer or elk	1	package wide egg noodles
1	chopped onion	1	pound processed cheese
	Salt and pepper		loaf
1	can whole kernel corn		Cracker crumbs
1	can tomatoes		

Brown meat and onion. Add salt, pepper, corn and tomatoes; simmer 15 minutes. Boil egg noodles; drain. In a 1½-quart casserole dish, make alternate layers of noodles, meat mixture and cheese. Top with cracker crumbs. Bake at 350 degrees until cheese melts.

POOR MAN'S STROGANOFF

Submitted by: Chad Schearer

1½	pounds elk hamburger	½	cup sour cream
1	onion, chopped	¼	teaspoon paprika
1	can cream of chicken soup	¼	cup butter
1	can mushrooms		Salt and pepper to taste

Sauté meat in butter until lightly brown. Add onion and brown. Blend together mushrooms and liquid, soup and sour cream. Pour over meat and onions. Cook until meat is tender. Serve over rice or egg noodles.

VENISON POT ROAST

Submitted by: Bill Jordan

4	pound venison roast	⅛	teaspoon ginger
2	bay leaves	¾	cup flour
1	medium garlic clove	½	cup vinegar
¾	teaspoon black pepper	¾	cup water
2	teaspoons salt	½	onion

Carefully trim roast from a young deer, of all tissue and hair. Place meat in a large bowl. Add vinegar and water to cover meat and place in refrigerator for 24 hours to marinate. Make ½-inch slits in roast with sharp knife and insert thin slices of garlic about every 2 inches. Moisten roast with shortening and roll in mixture of flour, salt, pepper and ginger until roast is covered. Add 2 tablespoons oil to a preheated cast iron skillet. Sear roast on all sides until browned. Remove roast. Add 1 cup hot water, onion and bay leaves. Place small rack in roaster; place meat on rack and cover. Cook in 300 degree oven until tender (about 2½ to 3½ hours) when tested with fork. When ready to serve, remove garlic slices and bay leaves. Make a gravy from the drippings by adding hot water to make sufficient amount along with 1 heaping tablespoon of remaining flour mixture per each cup of water added. Stir constantly until thickened as desired. Slice meat and serve.

THAI MARINATED VENISON RIBBONS

Submitted by: Kate Fiduccia

1	pound venison cutlets	2	cups water
½	cup chopped, fresh basil	1	cup beef broth (no salt added)
¼	cup reduced-sodium soy sauce	2	tablespoons reduced-sodium soy sauce
1	teaspoon minced garlic		
2	tablespoons crushed red pepper pods	2	cups cooked Ramen noodles in a small amount of the reserved cooking water (¼ cup)
2	teaspoons sugar		
2	teaspoons vinegar		
2	tablespoons peanut oil		

First trim all the fat and tallow from the meat. To make slicing the meat easier, partially freeze either the flank or the cutlets separately. Slice the venison diagonally across the grain into ¼-inch wide strips.

Combine the basil, soy sauce, minced garlic, crushed red pepper, sugar and vinegar into a large zip top plastic bag. Seal and shake well. Add the venison strips to the bag, seal and shake until the strips are thoroughly covered with marinade. Set the bag in the refrigerator for about 4 hours. Every now and then, turn the bag to keep the meat evenly coated.

Remove the meat from the bag and place on paper towel. Add a small amount of oil to a wok or large skillet. Heat the oil over medium/high heat for about 3 to 5 minutes. Add the venison and stir/flip to evenly cook the meat. Do not overload the pan as this will bring down the temperature of the oil and the meat will not cook properly. If necessary, cook small batches at a time and keep the venison on a warm platter after it has cooked.

After the meat is stir fried, toss in the noodles and liquid and stir. Place on a platter, garnish with scallions and serve immediately.

> *"The Great Spirit...created the buffalo, the deer, and other animals for food. He had scattered them over the country and taught us how to take them."*
>
> —Seneca Chief Red Jacket (1805)

VENISON ROAST

Submitted by: Jessica Larson

1	venison roast	1	can beef broth, beef
1	bay leaf		bouillon or consommé
	Seasoning salt		

Sprinkle roast liberally with seasoning salt. Put roast, bay leaf, and broth into pressure cooker. Pressure cook until tender, about 35 minutes.

Optional: After cooking, thicken broth with cornstarch to make gravy and serve over rice or potatoes.

VENISON LAROUX

Submitted by: Mike Roux

Cube three to four pounds of venison. Usually three or four steaks or chops will do. Marinate cubed meat in Italian salad dressing overnight in refrigerator in a sealed container.

To prepare, stir-fry marinated meat cubes, in the marinade in a skillet. Add two tablespoons dried minced onions. Drain meat after browning and place in deep baking dish. Stir in three cans cream of celery soup, one teaspoon garlic powder, and ½ cup grated cheddar cheese. Cover dish and bake for thirty minutes at 350 degrees.

Remove from oven, sprinkle top with diced green onion tops and spoon over boiled egg noodles.

Serves 6.

SKILLET FRIED DEER MEAT

Submitted by: Alex Rutledge

Flour	Seasoned salt
Onion	Garlic seasoning
Salt and pepper	Cola-flavored drink
Lemon pepper	Butter

Let deer meat soak in cola-flavored drink 30 minutes before rolling in flour. Season flour with ingredients to taste.

Heat iron skillet with butter until hot. After meat is ready to cook, cook real slow. Lay onion rings in bottom of skillet, then lay meat over onions. Turn meat every 3 minutes. This dish is great served with corn, green beans, fried tomatoes, and home made bread.

RAY EYE'S VENISON ROAST

Submitted by: Ray Eye

1	three to five pound venison roast	1½	cups of Johnny's Dry Rub (Buckhead Dry Rub may be substituted)
3	cups of Dale's Marinade (Buckhead Marinade may be substituted)		Apple juice Water

In a large covered bowl or pan, marinade the roast for a minimum of 4 hours. Remove roast from marinade but save remaining marinade and set aside. Liberally apply the dry rub to all sides of the roast.

Prepare the fire in your smoker. Use only wood charcoal. The charcoal pan should be ¾ full. Allow coals to burn until they are still whole but covered in gray ash. Place damp hickory chips on top of the coals.

Inside the smoker, fill the water pan with equal amounts of water and apple juice and then add remaining marinade. Place roast on top rack of the smoker and close the lid. Do not open for 4 hours. Your roast should be done and delicious.

SOUR CREAM AND ELK

Submitted by: Tad Brown

2	pounds elk steak, trimmed	2	beef bouillon cubes
2	large onions, chopped	1	(8 ounce) tub sour cream
1	large tomato, chopped	1	cup water
1	can mushrooms	2	tablespoon oil
1	brown gravy mix		Salt and pepper
			Garlic powder

Heat oil in skillet. Brown meat on high heat. Salt, pepper and garlic to taste. In large crock pot or slow cooker of some kind, add 1 cup water to brown gravy mix and 2 bouillon cubes on high heat. Move meat to crock pot with the gravy mix and bouillon. Add chopped onion and tomato. Cover and cook on high for about 4 to 5 hours, checking about every hour to see if water is needed. Stir and mix until meat is tender and mashes easily. Add mushrooms when heated. Add sour cream and serve over hot buttered rice with soy sauce to taste.

VENISON STEAKS IN SOY SAUCE

Submitted by: Chris Kirby

Thaw desired amount of venison steaks, preferably ½-inch thick; place in large bowl. Completely cover all venison with your favorite soy sauce, garlic salt, freshly ground pepper, two diced garlic cloves.

Heat charcoal to a good red hot cooking temperature. Lay your venison steaks about 3 to 4 inches above charcoal. Cook each side 5 minutes or until done.

Warning: Do not overcook venison steaks. It is very easy to overcook and dry out the meat. You want to make sure you cook the meat properly, but do not overcook.

WESTERN STYLE BAR-B-QUE VENISON CHOPS
Submitted by: Kate Fiduccia

6	venison chops, all fat trimmed	2	cups western style BBQ sauce

Western Style BBQ Sauce

½	cup white wine vinegar	1	teaspoon ground coriander
1	teaspoon red and black pepper	⅛	teaspoon paprika
¼	lemon, diced very fine	¼	teaspoon cayenne pepper
½	teaspoon ground cumin		

Combine all the above ingredients and let simmer for about 20 minutes.

EASY VENISON STEW
Submitted by: Ron Kruger

1	venison roast, about 2 pounds	Fresh carrots and potatoes
1	can cream of mushroom soup	Whole peppercorns and salt
1	can of cream of celery soup	1-2 large onions, chopped

Slice the venison roast against the grain and chop into chunks. Put in peppercorns, about one tablespoon of salt, the chopped onions and the venison meat. Cover with water. Cook this mixture on high for a couple of hours, then the rest of the day on low, or until the meat starts falling apart. Peel, wash and slice carrots and potatoes. Add to mixture. Add more salt if desired and more water if needed. Cook on high until vegetables are tender.

DEER STIR-FRY

Submitted by: Charlene Cooper

	Deer tenderloin or	1	cup broccoli, cut up
	ham steak	½	chopped onion
2	cups sliced carrots		Worcestershire sauce or
1½	cups sliced celery		soy sauce
½	cup sliced green pepper		Tomato, optional
1	cup cauliflower, cut up		

Slice deer meat into small chunks or thin strips. Spray wok with cooking spray. Heat wok until almost smoking. Place deer meat, healthy dash of Worcestershire or soy sauce, and onion into hot wok. Stir fry until deer meat is done.

Add rest of ingredients, except tomato, and stir fry on low until vegetables are tender crisp. If using a tomato, quarter the tomato and place in wok about 1 minute before serving. Serve over egg noodles or rice.

NOTE: Turkey breast or chicken works equally well.

VENISON STROGANOFF

Submitted by: Ted Nugent

2	pounds venison steaks	1	cup sour cream
1	envelope onion soup mix		Curry powder
	Fresh mushrooms		Garlic salt
1	Beef bouillon cube		Butter
	Cooking sherry		

Cut meat into thin strips (eliminating fat). Brown quickly in 3 tablespoons or more butter with mushrooms. Stir in ⅔ cup liquid (⅓ water, ⅓ sherry). Add the onion soup mix, a dash garlic salt, a dash of curry powder, and the bouillon cube, mix well, cover and simmer for 1½ hours or until meat is tender. Stir every 15 minutes, adding liquid when necessary. Just before serving, add sour cream and increase heat. Serve over rice or noodles for 4.

JIM'S BIG BUCK STROMBOLI

Submitted by: Jim Low

Combine in a large bowl and let stand for 10 minutes:

1	packet dry yeast	2	tablespoons olive oil
1	teaspoon salt	1	cup warm (not hot) water
1	teaspoon sugar		

Add:

2½	cups flour	1	tablespoon finely chopped, fresh sweet basil
2	tablespoons finely chopped sun-dried tomatoes		

Stir together by hand until flour is well moistened and then beat 20 strokes. Cover bowl with a towel and set in a warm place for 15 minutes.

Brown in a skillet:

½	tablespoon bacon grease	1	medium onion, chopped
½	pound ground venison		

Add:

½	cup water	1	teaspoon salt
1	teaspoon whole fennel seed	2-4	teaspoons red pepper flakes

Cook until most of water evaporates, leaving meat moist.

Roll dough out on a floured surface to form an oval ¼-inch thick. Top with:

	Venison/onion mixture	1	medium bell pepper, chopped
1	large ripe tomato, chopped	½	pound mozzarella cheese

Roll up dough along the long edge. Tuck open ends under. Brush with a beaten egg and sprinkle with sesame seeds. Place on a jelly roll pan and bake at 350 degrees until golden brown—30 to 40 minutes.

Serves two hungry people.

OLD-FASHIONED VENISON STEW

Submitted by: Stacey King

1½	cups water	2-3	pounds deer meat
½	cup beer	3	tablespoons vegetable oil
2	beef bouillon cubes	1	bay leaf
2	tablespoons flour	6	carrots, cut into 1-inch
1	tablespoon brown sugar		pieces
¼	teaspoon ground thyme	6	medium potatoes, cut
1	large onion, chopped		into 1-inch cubes
3	cloves garlic	1	cup frozen peas

In small mixing bowl, blend water, beer, bouillon cubes, flour, brown sugar, and thyme. Set aside. Remove all fat and silverskin from meat. Cut into 1-inch pieces. In Dutch oven, sauté onion and garlic in oil until tender; add deer meat and brown over medium-high heat. Add beer mixture and bay leaf to Dutch oven. Reduce heat; cover. Simmer until meat is almost tender, 2 to 3 hours, stirring occasionally. Add carrots and potatoes; cover. Cook 1 hour longer or until tender. Add peas; cover. Cook 10 minutes longer. Discard bay leaf before serving. Makes 6 to 8 servings.

SWEET AND SOUR

Submitted by: Denny Brauer

2	pounds deer or elk steak cut into 1-inch cubes	1	teaspoon salt
		½	cup vinegar
2	tablespoons vegetable oil	½	cup light molasses or
1	(16 ounce can) tomato sauce		syrup
		2	cups sliced carrots
2	teaspoons chili powder	2	cups onion
2	teaspoons paprika	1	green pepper
¼	cup sugar		

Brown meat in oil. Put in slow cooker. Add all remaining ingredients and mix. Cook 6 to 7 hours on low or 4 hours on high. Serve over rice.

NORTHERN SURF & TURF

Submitted by: Bob Foulkrod

First: Make a fantastic shot on your Caribou, being extra cautious to take out both lungs. This allows the animal to perish very quickly.

Second: Take out the back straps and hang them in a black spruce for about 15 to 20 hours.

At this time, you will start your campfire using the drift wood that you picked up along the river or lake when you set up camp. Let the smoke drift upward on the back straps until the Northern lights come out. After the morning dew by Mother Nature, start your campfire for breakfast. The smoke from coffee and bacon will again rise onto the back straps.

During the day the Whiskey Jack can pick away at it! This will help tenderize! Return early that day to remove them from the black spruce and cut them ½-inch thick and lay them on a stainless steel plate with salt and pepper to taste. Let them sit until you return from fishing.

Only one fish is required due to the average Speckled Trout being five pounds. Immediately, upon catching your trophy, lay it on a flat rock that has been walked over by thousands of caribou and touched for the first time with human hands as you take out the fillets. Take these back to your campsite and sprinkle only with lemon pepper, putting them next to the caribou fillets. Once again, start your fire. In your favorite pan, pour in cooking oil or lard, letting it get very hot.

As the Northern Sun is going down, you drop the fish in for approximately five minutes. As you take the fish out, lay them in pine bows to cool down while you are preparing the back straps. Don't leave these in too long, just a couple of minutes. These along with a fresh cup of water from the lake or river while watching the Northern lights and stars, will guarantee you to have the best surf and turf ever!

> *"The outdoors is cool."*
>
> —Bill Jordan

54

VENISON VEGETABLE SOUP

Submitted by: David Blanton

¾ pound venison, cubed
1 tablespoon vegetable oil
1 cup chopped onion
1 (16 ounce) package
 frozen mixed vegetables
2 (14 to 15 ounce) cans
 peeled tomatoes,
 undrained and diced
2 cups cubed, peeled
 potatoes

2 cups water
1 tablespoon sugar
2 teaspoons beef bouillon
 granules
1 teaspoon seasoned salt
½ teaspoon seasoned
 pepper
½ teaspoon garlic powder
¼ teaspoon hot sauce

In a Dutch oven or large 4 quart pot, brown the venison in oil. Add the onion, cover and simmer for ten minutes on medium-low heat. Add remaining ingredients, cover and simmer for 1 hour or longer until the venison is tender.

VENISON AND RED WINE STEW

(a.k.a. Pass the Buck)

Submitted by: Nick Muckerman

2-2½ pounds venison, cut into
 1½- inch cubes
6 tablespoons flour
1 teaspoon salt
¼ teaspoon pepper
2½ tablespoons vegetable oil
2 medium onions, diced
2-3 cloves garlic, mashed and
 chopped

1 cup spaghetti sauce
1 teaspoon dried basil
1 teaspoon dried thyme
4 ounces (½ cup) red wine
½ cup beef stock
1 cup baby carrots
1 cup diced potatoes

Combine flour, salt, and pepper in reclosable plastic bag or shallow dish. Shake or roll venison cubes in flour mixture. Heat oil in large skillet over medium-high heat. Add venison cubes and cook until browned and crisp. Remove meat from skillet. Add onion and garlic; sauté until translucent. Return venison to pan and remaining ingredients, except carrots and potatoes. Reduce heat and simmer for 1 hour. Add carrots and potatoes; continue to simmer for 30 minutes or until meat and vegetables are tender.

BUTTERFLY VENISON
Submitted by: Bob McNally

This was a favorite recipe of A.J. McClane, the late, great Field & Stream *Magazine gourmet, and a close family friend. It's my all-time favorite.*

1½	cups olive oil	1	tablespoon meat
½	cup oil		tenderizer
3	tablespoons soy sauce	4-6	garlic cloves (chopped
1	tablespoon seasoned salt		fine, or through a press)
1	tablespoon paprika		Juice of 1-2 whole lemons

This is my favorite way of eating venison. Take a ham (steak or back strap, too). Bone it so there are thick pieces and thin pieces. Marinate the whole piece of boned meat overnight. Cook on hot coals, like doing a steak. It will flame and you'll think it's burning, but it's not. Takes about 30 minutes for rare, big pieces. This is great for guests as there are well-done, medium and rare cuts of meat from a boned ham. The same recipe also is outstanding for elk, moose, caribou, and lean domestic meats like lamb and goat.

This meat is superb with grilled, whole onions. I use whole Vidalias. Well before you grill the meat, do the onions, whole, right on the fire. Takes about 30 minutes. Grill them black and then do the meat. When ready to serve, "pop" the inside steamed onion out of the black husks with a hot glove, and it is great with the meat.

Serve with a nice dry red wine, and toast the meal to A.J. McClane. It's also great cold, in sandwiches, like beef. This venison is so good, that I eat it this way before my first bowhunt of the season—makes me sure not to miss—much.

Camper's Stew
'Cause cookin' lak religion is—
Some's selected, an' some ain't,
An' rules don't no mo' mek a cook
Den sermons mek a saint.

—Author Unknown

TENDERLOIN SUPREME

Submitted by: Mark Drury

2	pounds deer loin	1	cup soy sauce
1	pound bacon		Toothpicks

Trim loin and cut into walnut size pieces. Cut bacon in thirds and wrap pieces of loin with bacon. Secure with toothpicks. Marinade in soy sauce 15 minutes; turn over for 15 minutes on the other side. Heat oven broiler to 350 degrees. Broil 3 minutes on each side and serve.

WHITETAIL STROGANOFF

Submitted by: Steve Stoltz

4	venison steaks (or 6 chops)	5	tablespoons of Worcestershire sauce
1	pound of thick sliced bacon	1	cup of diced celery, optional
1	cup of flour	1	(12 ounce) bag of broad egg noodles
1	large onion, diced		
3	medium size fresh tomatoes, chopped		

Slice venison into 2-inch wide strips or squares. In large, deep cast iron frying pan, fry a pound of bacon until crisp, then remove and let drain. Lightly flour both sides of venison chunks and place in hot bacon grease (using same frying pan). Brown both sides of meat, approximately 5 minutes each side. Let meat simmer in bacon grease and add diced onion, tomatoes, and celery on top of meat. Then pour approximately 5 tablespoons of Worcestershire sauce over entire dish. Cover and let simmer for approximately 1 hour. Boil egg noodles and drain. Serve this dish over the egg noodles.

Serve this meal with buttermilk biscuits and fresh green onions from the garden. Sprinkle bacon bits over this dish after completed.

WHITETAIL BLUES

Submitted by: Dawn Charging

1	package of venison steaks, ½-inch thick and 3 to 4 inches long	Thick slices of smoked bacon
	Coarse ground pepper	Skewers
	Bottle of burgundy wine	Casserole dish or pan
1	package of blue cheese	long enough to hold
1	bottle of blue cheese salad dressing	skewers and meat

Pound fillets to make steaks pliable enough to roll and skewer. Cover fillets and marinade in burgundy wine for several hours. Season mixture with coarse ground pepper and minced garlic cloves.

Roll fillets out. Sprinkle generous amount of blue cheese crumbs on meat. Roll cheese mixture up and wrap thick slices of bacon around the meat and cheese. Skewer and continue to roll meat and cheese until you have the portions you need to feed your family.

Pour the wine mixture into the pan to partially cover the meat and bacon rolls. Cover and bake for about ½ hour, basting the meat with the wine mixture. Keep meat liquid while baking, add more wine if needed. The blue cheese will melt into the wine mixture and appear to separate while cooking. When the meat is done, remove from pan and stir the wine and cheese mixture until it mixes well. Serve over the top of meat for a tasty dinner. Use bottled blue cheese dressing on the side as an additional meat dip for extra flavor.

> *"For unless a man inquires into the many factors that have brought him and his game together, he is only a gunner and not a hunter. If he does not know his quarry—its life cycle, the process of its reproduction, the course of its migrations, and the subtlety of its relationship to other creatures and its environment—its death means only marksmanship. Such a man reads only the last chapter of a mystery."*
>
> —Charles F. Waterman

WILD BOAR CHOPS
Submitted by: Ted Nugent

Only a few campers are fortunate enough to enjoy this delicious game meat; the rest must be content with domestic pork chops. But if you should bag a wild boar, serve it this way.

Salt and pepper 4 chops, sprinkle with flour and brown well on both sides in 3 tablespoons of hot fat. Core (but do not peel) 2 pounds of apples and cut in thick slices. Put a dash of paprika and 6 raisins on top of each browned chop. Then cover with the apple slices, 2 tablespoons of brown sugar and ¼ cup of hot water. Cover skillet and simmer until well done, about 40 minutes. Cook 1 large or 2 small chops per person.

Prayer of a Hunter's Wife

Grant me patience, Lord, I pray
When the alarm rings out to start the day...
And yet it's only three a.m.,
And it's ringing to awaken HIM
For I'm married to a hunter, Lord,
And I never could decide
Just why he hunts when it's so dark
Or when it's "pouring down" outside.
But I guess that all those deer he missed
Or the turkey he let get away
Would never have approached at all
If it had been a sunny day.
And, Lord, I ask for nimble hands
When it's time to clean those birds
Or when it comes to cooking things
I can't describe with words.
I'm not asking You to change him, Lord,
For he's a hunter to the core
All I need is a little patience
'Cause I couldn't love him more!

—Author Unknown

THE HUNTING TRADITION—PASSING IT ON

Having grown up with a wildlife biologist for a father, I learned at an early age that the natural world offers more than picnic spots and ski slopes. I was never taught to fear animals, but to respect their natural wildness and keep a safe distance from the ones that could bite or sting. Rattlesnakes, porcupines and scorpions all held my attention, and I was allowed to be fascinated by them, never realizing until years later the careful watch over me that my dad kept.

Nature continued to captivate me as I grew up. Last winter, I went deer hunting for the first time. I was drawn to hunting not only by the lure of good venison dinners, but also by years of Dad's tales of crawling across Wyoming prairies after pronghorn and spending bone-chilling nights in camp during elk season. These stories intrigued me, and I hungered to share in some of his accounts of failure and success.

Early one December morning we drove in the dark to the deer lease. My heart raced ahead of us, and I fretted silently at what might happen when I was alone in a tree stand. Dad was nervous too, but his caring was evident in small ways, like the toe-warming packets he got for my boots and the matching camouflage head covers purchased for us weeks earlier.

Once settled in my tree stand, I relaxed, reassured that my father's stand was only a few hundred yards away. I forgot the morning chill as I watched squirrels, listened to birds, and even spotted a grey fox picking its way through the forest. My buck license kept me from trying for any of the several does that ambled by, so I just watched them intently, my heart thundering.

Finally, two bucks emerged, one a nice eight-point. I followed them with my rifle through the woods, but never could seem to get a clear shot—brambles appeared from nowhere like hands blocking my view. The two deer made it safely out of my range and disappeared.

Later, my dad told me he had seen the same two bucks, but didn't shoot so that I'd have a chance. Disappointed with myself, I felt bad that my father missed out on a deer for my sake, and wished aloud that I had taken a shot. Dad said he was proud that I didn't shoot when I wasn't certain of my target. My wounded pride healed a bit at his praise, and the thrill of being out in the woods—alone, but with someone I loved nearby—was indescribable.

I plan to hunt for the rest of my life—and not just because I've learned its value in managing wildlife, but because my father has made it a part of me. He's shown me that good hunters respect wildlife, and the trophy isn't always a kill. And, years from now, when I see the glow of love for wilderness in my own child's eyes, I'll know he's close.

—Jessica Larson

Freshwater

GENERATIONS OF TRADITION

GENERATIONS OF TRADITION

Dedicated to George Van Patten, my grandfather.
March 31, 1907-April 11, 1998

The drive to town dragged on for an eternity for the young boy from the country. This was the day his grandpa promised to take him into town to buy his first fly rod. The store was spacious and not well lit, but the boy knew where the rack stood which held his fly rod. The boy had saved his money from the odd jobs he had done for his grandparents and the neighbors from the surrounding farms. In his pocket was fifteen dollars, fifteen hard-earned dollars. Just enough to purchase the finest looking fly rod he had ever laid his young eyes on.

The scene took place over thirty years ago, yet it is just as clear in my mind as it was that day. I remember the trip back to the farm. I planned fishing trips with Gramps and daydreamed of the lunkers that would succumb to my new rod. The car hadn't stopped in the drive until I was running hard to the house to grab my meager collection of popping bugs and made a mad dash for the pond. My hands were shaking with excitement as I tried to tie on a fly. I stood at the side of the pond for a moment before I made my first cast soaking in the feeling of this fine fishing implement. The weight of the reel at the end of the rod seemed to balance perfectly in my small hand. Here it was in my hand. Right here at my pond. Gosh, it really was mine now.

Stripping line from the reel, I began my first cast. The line shot out over the water's surface and dropped gently as a feather laying the fly next to a partially submerged log. Before I could start the popping retrieve, the water exploded with a fury of flashing green and gold. I raised the rod to set the hook and felt the power of the fish struggling to free itself. In a moment, it was over. The fish came to me. I held it up to admire for a second in the sunlight. The contrast of color etched a memory in the recesses of my mind that would last a lifetime. The green of the fish against the powder blue of the sky, and the bright yellow and gold from my fly rod seemed to swirl together for a moment. Probably it was the tears of pure joy. Embarrassed, I turned at a sound behind me. There stood my grandfather, smiling with a pride only a grandfather can know. He urged me to release the fish unharmed that I might catch it another day.

I couldn't believe what I was hearing. Turn it loose? The first fish I had caught on my new fly rod? Was my grandfather serious? I wanted to take it home, perhaps have it mounted or something. Granted, it wasn't a big fish, but it was the first on my new rod. Reluctantly, I returned the fish to the water. It stayed at the edge of the pond in the shallow water for a few seconds giving me a last look before it darted off to a cool spot under a log somewhere. This time the tears in my eyes weren't from joy, but sadness. Quickly I wiped them away so my grandfather wouldn't see them. He called to me to come sit by him on an old tree stump and explained to me about the importance of catching and releasing fish to ensure there would always be fish to catch.

What my grandfather taught me that day made a lot of sense and thirty-some years later, I'm still releasing the majority of the fish I catch to re-catch on another day. That old fiberglass fly rod still hangs on the front porch at my grandparents' home. My children have dragged that old rod down to the pond many times over the years, reliving for me that summer day many years ago.

The cork on the handle is nearly gone and the line is stiff and cracked, but it will still catch a sunfish or a bass from the pond. Who knows, maybe my son or daughter will give that same lecture to their children on that same tree stump, if it's still there. Passing on to another generation the lesson my grandfather taught to me.

My grandfather is gone now. I believe he left me with the answer to one of the reasons for our existence: To believe in something and pass it on to the next generation. Thus, creating a tradition, leaving something memorable for each new generation to hold and carry on.

—Mark Van Patten

Editor's Note: Gramps would be proud of Mark. Mark's love of fishing and Ozark streams has led him down fruitful paths. Mark's leadership brought about a clean-up effort on Roubidoux Creek in Pulaski County, Missouri. That group eventually became the first Stream Team in the state. Mark became the first Stream Team Coordinator for the Conservation Federation of Misouri.

The Stream Team program has won numerous regional and national honors. Mark is now the Fisheries Coordination Biologist with the Missouri Department of Conservation. Mark, Gramps is proud!!!

CAMPFIRE BAKED TROUT

Submitted by: Ron Kruger

1	pink-fleshed trout of 3 to	1	ripe red tomato
	4 pounds		Butter
4-6	strips of slab bacon		Salt and pepper

Lay cleaned trout on large sheet of aluminum foil. Rub the trout inside and out with butter and sprinkle with salt and pepper. Lay a bacon strip on each side of the inside cavity and stuff the middle with tomato wedges and pats of butter. Then lay a strip of bacon lengthwise under and above the trout and close the foil. If cooking in a campfire, use at lease six complete wraps of foil and submerge it in hot coals for about 20 minutes, or until foil maintains a depression when squeezed with tongs. If baking in the oven, use three complete coverings of foil and place in a baking dish. Cook at 450 degrees for ½ hour.

FLORIDA FISH CAMP BASS BOIL

Submitted by: Virgil Ward

Clean and fillet enough bass to feed the camp visitors. Roll fillets in beer batter. Salt to taste. Heat large iron kettle full of cooking oil, heated by a propane burner. Bring oil to a boil, drop in fillets. When they come to the top of the oil, they are ready to eat.

SMOKED BARBEQUE CATFISH

Submitted by: Bill Dance

6	cleaned, skinned catfish (roughly 1½ to 2 pounds each) Butter flavored salt	28	Pepper ounces of hickory smoked barbeque sauce Seasoned salt

Clean whole, skinned fish. Salt well inside and out with seasoned salt and a small amount of black pepper. Pack the catfish tightly in a large rotisserie basket, as naturally, they'll shrink during cooking. In a covered grill, heat coals to approximately 400 degrees. Smoke the fish for 1 hour at a high temperature, and then reduce the heat to 350 degrees for another hour. During the last 30 minutes of cooking, baste with the barbeque sauce a couple of times.

Serves 6 to 8.

I'm sure you've heard the expression, "Shoofly pie and apple pan dowdy makes your eyes light up and your stomach say howdy." Well, this one will, too!

CAJUN MUSTARD STRIPER

Submitted by: Bill Fletcher

1	10 to15 pound ocean striper Hot, creamy Cajun mustard	Yellow cornmeal Cooking oil

Cube striper fillets into 1-inch cubes. Chill thoroughly and dip in Cajun mustard. Roll in yellow cornmeal and deep fry at 350 degrees. Drain on an absorbent cloth. Eat while hot.

BLUEGILL GUY PAN

Submitted by: Keith Kavajecz

This is a quick little recipe for preparing fish in a wok. I have used walleye, bluegill, perch, white bass and many other thinly cut, not too fatty fish. Guy or Gy is the Chinese word for chicken. I just use it here because my kids liked the sound of it.

2	cups fish fillets (maximum thickness should be about ¼ inch)	1	tablespoon oriental sauce
		¼	cup oil (less may be needed)
2	tablespoons soy sauce	½	tablespoon garlic salt

Coat with oil an electric wok or frying pan at high temperature. Add fish, soy sauce, and garlic salt. Brown fish - attempt to keep fillets intact by flipping the fish like a pancake. Add oriental sauce; cover and cook 5 minutes, turning once.

The dish can be served with rice or potatoes and will have a nice, dark gravy with it.

CANNED CARP

Submitted by: Mike McClelland

Fillet fish; remove skin, bones and red meat from carp. Cut into pieces about 1-inch wide and two inches long.

Pack raw fish into pint jars leaving one inch head-room and add to each jar: 1 teaspoon salt, 3 teaspoons white vinegar, 1 to 3 drops of red food coloring. Process in pressure cooker for 90 minutes per 10 pounds of fish. Works with carp, northern pike and freshwater drum.

CERVICHE
A Fish Appetizer

Submitted by: Jim Dougherty

1	pound white fish (crappie fillets are excellent)	1	tablespoon vinegar (red wine)
1	cup lime juice	¼-½	diced Ortega pepper
1	onion	1½	teaspoons oregano
2	tomatoes		Salt and pepper
4	tablespoons vegetable oil	1	avocado

Cut fish into cubes (approximately ½-inch); add lime juice. Soak until fish loses translucent look. The juice is cooking the fish. Pour off juice. Dice half onion fine. Dice tomatoes and add fish. Sprinkle mixture with oil, vinegar, chiles, oregano, salt and pepper. Refrigerate 3 to 4 hours. Garnish with other onion half, add cubed avocado. Serve with crackers or tortilla chips as a dip.

FISH DUMPLINGS
Submitted by: Rick Olson

1	pound white fish	¼	cup whipping cream
¼	cup shrimp		Salt and pepper to taste
2	egg whites		

Blend all ingredients together. Form little balls and drop them into a kettle of boiling salt water. Remove them when they float, and serve with white sauce. (I use a food processor to blend ingredients).

TROUT STUFFED WITH CRABMEAT

Submitted by: Shirley Grenoble

This is the recipe I use when I'm going to make trout for company. These ingredients make enough for four 12-inch trout. Adjust the amounts given to the number and size of trout you are preparing.

3	stale rolls or several pieces of stale bread	8	ounces crabmeat
1	cup milk		Pinch of oregano
1	egg		Juice of half a lemon
⅓	cup chopped, raw bacon	2	dashes Worcestershire sauce
⅓	cup chopped, raw onion		Salt and pepper

Split and bone trout but do not separate the halves. To prepare the stuffing, soak bread in milk, squeeze dry and add egg. Sauté bacon and onions until onions are limp but not brown. Add the crabmeat and sauté for five minutes. Add to bread mixture then stir in remaining ingredients.

Spread the stuffing on ½ of each trout and fold the other half on top. Sprinkle top of trout with paprika and brush with melted butter. Bake in 400 degree oven until skin is brown and crisp.

OVEN FRIED CRAPPIE FILLETS

Submitted by: Virgil Ward

Use one pound of crappie fillets. Roll them in lemon-lime soda batter. Place them on non-stick baking dish. Bake in preheated oven at 450 degrees for 12 minutes or until fillets flake easily when tested with a fork.

CRAPPIE FISH SALAD

Submitted by: Bill Dance

2-4	8-ounce fillets	3	tablespoons dill pickles, diced
	Dash butter flavored salt		
	Dash of pepper	3	tablespoons onion, chopped (optional)
3	tablespoons mayonnaise		
3	tablespoons diced celery		

Cook fillets in a microwave oven for 2½ to 3 minutes at a high setting. Determine if fish is cooked by placing a fork into the meat. The fillets should flake. Sprinkle fillets with butter flavored salt and pepper.

Once cooled, place the fillets in a 2-quart mixing bowl and add mayonnaise, diced celery, dill pickles, onions. Mix together. Serve with lettuce leaves in a dinner salad, as an appetizer or use for sandwiches.

Serves 4-6.

I don't know how good this one might sound to you, but I'll promise you my favorite rod and reel if you ever try it once, you'll never forget it. You'll definitely have to serve it again. It's delicious!

FISH, TURKEY & CHICKEN

Submitted by: Jerry Martin

Cut into strips ½-inch thick. Dip in buttermilk and roll in breading. Breading should consist of:

4	ounces crushed cornflakes	1	teaspoon salt
4	ounces flour	1	teaspoon lemon pepper

Deep fry at 360 degrees until done.

FAT CAT MULLIGAN

Submitted by: Keith Sutton

3	bacon slices, diced	1	tablespoon salt
3	medium onions, sliced thin	2	teaspoons freshly ground black pepper
2	pounds catfish fillets, cut in bite-size pieces	3	cups boiling water
2	pounds potatoes, diced	3½	cups chopped canned tomatoes
½	teaspoon celery seed	2	tablespoons fresh parsley, chopped fine
2	large carrots, diced		
¼	cup diced green bell pepper		

Sauté bacon in a deep kettle until lightly browned, then remove bacon bits and set aside. Sauté onion slices in bacon grease until tender. Stir in fish, potatoes, celery seed, carrots, green pepper, salt, black pepper and water. Simmer, covered, until vegetables are tender, about 30 minutes. Add tomatoes, and heat through. Garnish with chopped parsley and bacon bits.

FISH BAKE

Submitted by: Rick Olson

1	cup chopped onion		Salt and pepper to taste
½	cup chopped celery and tops	¼	cup vegetable oil
½	cup chopped parsley	2	cans tomato sauce
2	pounds fish fillets		

Combine onion, celery, parsley, pour into a shallow baking dish. Place fish fillets in overlapping layers over the vegetables. Salt and pepper. Pour oil over the fish. Bake at 375 degrees for 10 minutes Pour tomato sauce over all of the ingredients and bake at 350 degrees for 30 to 35 minutes.

WALLEYE CHILI

Submitted by: Rick Olson

4-5	pounds walleye	2	cups horseradish
2	quarts ketchup	1	cup wine sauce
2	(51 ounce) cans tomato soup	2	teaspoons hot sauce
		2-3	cups onions, diced
1-2	cups lemon juice		Add chili powder,
2	large green peppers, diced		oregano, garlic powder to taste

Cut fish into small bite-size pieces. Sauté fish separately. Sauté diced vegetables, then add ketchup and other ingredients. Add fish chunks, and simmer for 1 hour over low heat.

This makes a very large batch!

FISH CHOWDER

Submitted by: Bill Dance

4-5	slices of bacon; crisp, broken into pieces	1	teaspoon salt
2	medium onions, sliced	4	cups milk
2	cups sliced Irish potatoes	4	cups water
2	tablespoons butter or margarine	2	pounds cubed, boneless fillets

Bring to boil: bacon, onions, potatoes, salt, in 4 cups of water. Reduce heat and simmer 10 to 15 minutes. When potatoes are nearly soft, put in cubed fillets. Cook fish until tender (about 15 minutes). Add milk and butter. Bring to boil and simmer until soup is hot. Salt and pepper to taste.

†David Besenger ©1998

FISHING WITH ST. NICK

FISHING WITH SAINT NICK

The weather was typical for December. The thermometer registered a cold thirty-four degrees, and the unpredictable guy on the weather channel was predicting six or more inches of snow by tomorrow afternoon. It did not matter. I was going fishing in spite of the impending forecast.

Loading my gear in the truck that morning, I felt anxious, almost nervous. It started spitting a skiff of snow across the windshield of the truck as I turned out of my driveway. My destination was a small secluded stream somewhere in Phelps County Missouri.

Winter has always been my favorite time of the year to fish. The usual crowds are now at home in their warm living rooms watching football on TV, leaving the stream deserted and peaceful. By the time I struggled into my waders, the snowfall had increased in intensity and was beginning to accumulate on the ground. There was no wind blowing. The snow was silently falling, covering the banks of the stream with the wet stuff. The water looked like an antique mirror, dark, yet reflective. Standing at streamside, the beauty of this wintery scene nearly took my breath.

After an hour of blissful fishing solitude, I rounded a bend in the stream. There I noticed a small red glow through the curtain of white. Wading toward the glow, it soon became apparent that it was the warm light from an angler's pipe. The fisherman had not noticed me, so I halted my approach and took up a position out of sight to observe. As I watched this fellow light his pipe, a ring of smoke encircled his head like a Christmas wreath. He was very short, with a belly that filled his waders to capacity. He was an elderly gentleman, I presumed by the length of his snow-white beard. His cast was that of a master, perfect poetry.

With an air of confidence, his fly landed precisely where it should. In no more than a four count he had a 16-inch wild rainbow trout fighting the pressure from his expert line handling. In what seemed like a wink of an eye the trout succumbed and gracefully slid to the angler's hand. A grin from one rosy cheek to the other showed his love for the fish as he gently removed the hook and let the fish slip back to its home. He stood up to inspect his fly, and I got a good look at his face. It was round with an elfish look; his eyes were wise, as if he had seen centuries pass. There was something very familiar about this short, chubby gentleman. I just could not put my finger on it.

I was beginning to feel uneasy about intruding on the angler's solitude from behind his back. So I let him know of my presence, wading toward him. The fisherman seemed as surprised to see me out in this weather as I was to see him. With a voice as smooth as silk he turned and spoke. "Another brother of the angler to share in a glorious winter day of fishing. Have you had the luck of the season on your line today?" I replied that I had caught a few small fish, but was content just to be on the stream. I extended my hand and introduced myself inquiring as to his name, to which he simply replied, "Nick."

We talked flies, favorite streams and our common love of the bamboo fly rod for nearly an hour. Nick had a strange way of talking, old country maybe. His knowledge of fly fishing antiquity intrigued me, as this subject was one of my favorites.

Graciously, the gentleman begged to be excused from our meeting. He had a pressing appointment somewhere up north. As Nick left the stream, climbing the bank with the agility of a young man, he turned once more in my direction. He pointed to a root wad directly in front of me and indicated if I were to cast a Telico Nymph upstream and let the current take it down into the undercut, I might catch a nice fish. I thanked him for the information and did what he suggested. As soon as the fly drifted under the root wad, my line straightened. He was right. I turned to tell Nick thanks again but he was gone as if he had disappeared into thin air. The fish gave me a fight I would not soon forget. The struggle between man and fish went on for time forgotten. Exhausted, the fish came to my shaking hand. The rainbow was 27 inches long and had to weigh more than nine pounds. A true trophy!

As I admired this beautiful specimen something strange caught my eye. Tied to the fish's tail was a big red ribbon, the kind you find on a package under the Christmas tree. There was some writing on the ribbon in silver glitter. I looked closer to make out what it said and a lump rose in my throat: The silver glitter spelled out a message. "Merry Christmas, Brother. Thanks for the company."

—Mark Van Patten

FISH PATTIES

Submitted by: Rick Olson

5	pounds walleye fillets, diced	½	medium onion, chopped
2	eggs	¼	medium green pepper, chopped
1	cup pancake flour or biscuit baking mix	¾	cup milk

Beat the eggs, then stir them together with the other ingredients. The mixture should have the consistency of potato salad. (Add a little milk if too dry, or biscuit baking mix if too moist). Preheat griddle to 325 degrees. Coat liberally with oil. Drop with large spoon full, and fry until golden brown, turning once. (Just like pancakes).

NO-FUSS QUICK-FRIED CRAPPIE

Submitted by: Tim Huffman

Crappie fillets	Corn meal
Salt	Shortening (called grease
Pepper	by real fishermen)

Wash fillets, drain. Salt and pepper to taste. Add a pinch of ground red pepper (optional). Roll in cornmeal while fillets are still moist. Drop into hot grease. Cook to desired browness; usually about three minutes. Do not overcook.

TEMPURS

Submitted by: Casey Iwai

1	cup flour	1	teaspoon sugar
1	cup cold water	½	teaspoon baking powder
1	egg		

Mix egg, water, sugar and baking powder. Add flour. Dip pieces of firm-fleshed white fish (catfish, crappie, white bass are favorites) in batter and fry in vegetable oil.

FISH TACOS

Submitted by: Cheryl McDonald

Soft taco shells (corn or flour)		**Rice**
	1	**can stewed tomatoes**
Black beans		**Fresh dolphin or wahoo**
Onions		**(or your own personal**
Green and red peppers		**favorite)**
Jalapeño peppers		

Soak and cook 2 cups of black beans until soft. Cook rice as directed on package (white, brown or Spanish rice).

Sauté until soft, in large pan, the following:

Onions (cut in 1½-inch strips)

Peppers (cut into 1½-inch strips)

Jalapeño peppers (use as many as your personal "spicy" palate desires)

Add stewed tomatoes. Marinate fish in beer for one hour then wrap loosely in tin foil, bake for approximately 15 minutes at 350 degrees.

Combine:

Lay soft taco shell flat.

Cut fish into large size chunks and place on soft taco shell.

Add sauté mix of peppers, onions and tomatoes.

Add four tablespoons of black beans.

Fold bottom of soft taco (about ¼-inch) upward, then roll contents into the shell. Place the remaining black beans on the rice and mix.

"Forgive them, for they are anglers, and know not the meaning of truth."

—Acts of the Fisherman: 2:12

SKILLET FRIED GOGGLE-EYE

Submitted by: Alex Rutledge

Yellow cornmeal	Garlic salt
Filleted goggle-eye	Bacon grease
Lemon pepper	Lemon juice

Let goggle-eye soak in lemon juice and saltwater for 2 hours before preparing.

Heat iron skillet until grease is hot. Roll fillets in yellow cornmeal seasoned to taste with lemon pepper and garlic salt. Cook fillets until crispy brown or to taste. Serve fish with bar-b-que sauce. Try it; you'll like it!

FROG LEGS MORNAY

Submitted by: Keith Sutton

8	medium frog legs	1	clove garlic, finely
2	tablespoons white wine		minced
1	cup medium white sauce	4	tablespoons sliced
⅓	cup shredded Gruyère		mushrooms
	cheese		Parmesan cheese
¼	cup cream or half-and-		
	half, whipped		

To make a quick Mornay sauce, mix wine, white sauce, and Gruyère cheese in a pan, and heat until the cheese is melted. Fold in the cream. Sauté the frog legs in butter along with the garlic, until the legs are lightly browned. Place four legs in each of two greased individual casserole dishes. Arrange two tablespoons of mushrooms, which have been sautéed in butter, over the legs in each dish. Pour Mornay sauce over the mushrooms, and sprinkle the top of each casserole with shredded or grated Parmesan cheese. Slip under the broiler to brown. Serve hot.

TOM'S FROG LEGS

Submitted by: Tom Evans

1	egg beaten with fork
1	pound of frog legs
2	cups flour or enough to coat legs
¼	cup oil
½	cup white cooking wine
1	medium garlic clove, minced

Pinch of salt
Pinch of black pepper
(fresh ground)
Pinch of paprika
1   package yellow rice

Prepare rice as directed. While rice is cooking, add seasonings to egg. Cover frog legs in egg mixture then roll in flour. Preheat oil in cast iron skillet on medium heat. Put coated frog legs in pan and brown, no lid. When finished, leave legs in skillet and pour off remaining oil. Add cooking wine and garlic to skillet. Cover and simmer for 30 minutes. Serve frog legs over bed of rice, spooning some of the juices over the top.

GARFISH MISSISSIPPI

Submitted by: Keith Sutton

1	slab of gar meat (6 inches wide, 8 to 10 inches long, ¾-inch thick)	½	cup green onions, chopped
1	(15-ounce) bottle ketchup	1	tablespoon salt
¼	cup hot sauce	2	teaspoons fresh, ground black pepper
½	cup celery, chopped	2	cups water
1	onion, chopped	1	lemon
4	tablespoons soy sauce		

Mix all ingredients, except the meat and lemon, in a large shallow glass baking dish. Add the meat, cover and marinate overnight in the refrigerator. The next day, stir it up and place in a 400 degree oven for about one hour. Check the dish twice during cooking, and spoon juice over the meat. Squeeze lemon juice on the meat before serving.

SMOKED GRASS CARP
Submitted by: Jim Low

Take a 10-pound grass carp, scale and remove head and entrails. Wipe fish dry inside and out. Using a table fork, make perforations through skin well into meat. Sprinkle liberally with lemon juice inside and out and coat all surfaces with ground black pepper and dried, granulated garlic.

Light charcoal and arrange at one end of a covered barbecue grill. Place half a dozen water-soaked 1- by 1-inch sticks of sassafras wood on the charcoal. Sections of sapling are perfect. Place fish at opposite end of grill so it cooks by indirect heat. Cover grill and cook until exterior of fish is mahogany brown and meat is loose and flaky all the way to the back bone. This may take 2 to 4 hours, depending on grill temperature. Longer is better, but don't cook so long that the meat dries out.

Remove fish from grill and allow to cool at room temperature. Remove skin and discard. Remove meat from carcass in one-inch cubes, removing forked bones as you go. Place meat in a storage container and chill.

Grass carp flesh has a firm, meaty texture, mild, sweet flavor and freezes well. The bones are large and easy to find.

For delicious fish sandwiches, toast a Kaiser roll, slather with tartar sauce and add warm meat. Top with a slice of American cheese and serve.

Also excellent in casseroles or prepared as you would for tuna salad.

MICROWAVE FISH
Submitted by: Tony Allbright

Place bass fillets on a dish (like a microwave bacon pan). Put a pat of butter on top of each fillet. You can use your imagination, such as lemon pepper, salsa, cheese, Parmesan cheese, etc. to top the fish. Microwave for 7 to 8 minutes, depending on your microwave.

NIGHT MANEUVERS

Trees whipped past my face as I cruised along the gravel road. Even with the ATV's light on, I found it hard to see through the mist in the darkness of the warm, summer night. I slowed down as I neared a creek crossing. Although we were frog gigging, our gigging group had better places to go than a clear, spring creek.

We rode on until we came to the farmer's entrance gate. Luke Halbert, a new friend I had recently met while vacationing on a farm near Steelville, Missouri, had asked permission to gig in the farmer's pond. He opened the gate as the rest of our group rode through. Justin Halbert, Luke's cousin, led us to a large pond. One side of the pond was covered with tall grass and weeds (a good place to find frogs), and the other side was a mixture of large rocks and mud banks. We got off and turned on our flashlights. I had a hand-held waterproof light while Luke and my friend Greg Grimes had powerful head lights. We approached the pond slowly. We decided to break up into two large groups of two, Luke and I and Greg and Justin.

We slowly and quietly walked along the bank, while shining the lights in front of us. "Stop," Luke whispered. "Do you see him?"

"No," I replied.

"Look right in the middle of my light," Luke instructed.

"I still can't see him"...KERPLUNK. The frog plopped into the water. "Oh, now I see him." I looked at the dark green head that was slightly above the water.

The frog's eyes are what gives it away. They usually glow when the light hits them. They're hard to spot at first, but once you get used to it, it's easy.

We continued a few more yards until Luke spotted another one. "Do you see it?"

"Keep the light on him and watch how I gig him," Luke told me. He stalked his way up to the frog. When he got within reach, he eased the gig to within about three inches from the frog. Then he thrust the five-pronged gig into the frog.

I walked over to Luke while he put the big bullfrog in a large bag. We crept along the bank until we spotted another frog. This time, it was my turn. While Luke held the light, I silently stalked the frog. Finally I was within range. I put the gig behind his head and...KERPLUNK, another frog escaped! "This is harder than I thought," I told Luke as we walked further along the bank.

Finally, we met up with Greg and Justin. "How many did you guys get?" we asked.

"Four," Justin responded. "How many did you get?"

"One, but he's really big," Luke told them.

"Let's go to the slough," Justin said, "that's the best place to gig around here."

We made our way back through the farmer's yard and to the gravel road. We were driving along the gravel road until light from my ATV caught Justin and his mini-bike standing motionless ahead of us. I slowed down to see what was going on. Justin pointed slowly in front of me and Greg. I looked over the front of my four-wheeler. I was shocked and scared by what I saw. There were two skunks standing right in front of the ATV. I froze. Eventually, they walked away, but I'm glad I slowed down. I would have been sleeping in the barn if I hadn't.

We continued on and before I knew it, I was standing at the muddy bank of a long, green, smelly, slimy, snake infested slough — perfect frog habitat. Greg and I took one side of the slough, while Luke and Justin walked on the other side. It was a great system. We stayed parallel as we walked along the edge of the slough. When one of us spotted a frog, the other side would put the light on it while we gigged it.

The beam from my light reflected off a frog sitting well beyond my reach, so I continued to scan for a closer target. "What are you doing?" cried Luke. "There's a perfectly good frog out there."

"But it's sitting in the middle of the slough."

"Wade out there and get him. Nothing to be afraid of," he told me.

"Easy for him to say," I thought, as I...GLOP, stepped into the water. I was knee-deep as I slowly advanced toward the frog. My mind was filled with thoughts of cottonmouths and giant alligator snapping turtles as I sunk waist-deep. The frog was now about 10 feet away from me. I tried my hardest not to cause any waves in the water. Finally, I was about five feet from the...GLUCK, I suddenly sunk chest-deep in the green moss of the slough. At last, I was within reach of my prey. I knew it would be impossible to get the frog from above so I eased the gig under him.

The frog was facing away from me. Greg had the light on him and the frog was clueless about what was going on. On the count of three, I thought. One...two...SMACK, the frog dove into the deep water. I looked up at Greg, who had jerked the light away. "What happened?" I asked.

"I couldn't help it. There was a mosquito on my neck," was his reply.

"Couldn't you have waited for just one more second?" I asked.

"It hurt," he replied.

We rode back to the house and cleaned the frogs. There's no special way to clean them, just get the skin off of their back legs and disconnect them from the rest of the body. Frog legs are a delicacy. I actually like to cook them myself as a treat for family and friends.

Jim "Pappy" Emerson, an Ozark hillbilly and famous outdoorsman, once took the time to teach me the following recipe:

½ cup flour   1 teaspoon lemon pepper
½ teaspoon pepper   butter, as needed

Mix all ingredients, except butter, in small bowl. Dredge frog legs in flour mixture. Melt butter in skillet, and add frog legs. Add butter as needed. Cook until legs appear white.

These are a great appetizer if you only have a few. They're a wonderful entree if you have enough to satisfy your appetite.

—Nick Muckerman

KWIK AND E-Z KING FISH

Submitted by: Boomer Sutton

Cut King mackerel into ½- to ¾-inch steaks.

Marinade in:

Italian salad dressing   **Granulated onions**
Seasoned salt   **Salt and pepper**
Worcestershire sauce

for at least 2 hours (preferably overnight).

Grill 10 minutes each side; serve with Cajun Potatoes.

LOW CHOLESTEROL STRIPER

Submitted by: Bill Fletcher

1	10-15 pound ocean striper		Water
	Lemon juice		Cocktail sauce

Cube striper fillets into 1-inch cubes and chill. Place 4 cubes into a pint freezer bag with 1 teaspoon of water. Add a few drops of lemon juice. Cook in a 400 watt microwave for 3 minutes. The bag will explode and the water will evaporate, steaming the striper cubes in the process. Serve with cocktail sauce.

PICKLED FISH

Submitted by: Mike McClelland

1	quart northern pike, cut into 1½-inch pieces	1	onion
		1	cup pickling salt
1	cup sugar	1	cup white wine
2-3	tablespoons mixed pickling spice	2¼	cups white vinegar

Boil one and a quarter cup white vinegar and salt. Try to dissolve some of the salt. Pour over fish. After they've cooled, put in refrigerator. Let sit 5 days, stirring occasionally. After 5 days, wash until clear. Put it into cold water for one hour. Drain well.

Cook 1 cup white vinegar and 1 cup sugar in a pan until dissolved. Let cool. Add 1 cup white wine, layer onion and fish in quart jar. (Use onions according to your liking). Put 2 or 3 tablespoons mixed pickling spice on top of jar. Pour syrup over all. Refrigerate. Will be ready to eat in 3 or 4 days. Store in refrigerator no longer than 4 weeks.

STUFFED RAINBOW TROUT
(a.k.a. Bows & Bacon)

Submitted by: Nick Muckerman

6	ounces bacon, diced	½	cup white wine
1	medium onion, finely diced		White pepper to taste (about ¼ teaspoon)
1	clove garlic, finely diced	¼	cup bread crumbs
½	pound (8 ounces) ham, finely diced	6	whole boneless rainbow trout (about 10 to 12 ounces each)
1	tablespoon chopped, fresh parsley	2	tablespoons butter, cut into 6 pats
1½	teaspoons dried basil		
1½	teaspoons dried tarragon		

Preheat oven to 375 degrees. In medium sauté pan, cook bacon until crisp. Remove bacon from pan and set aside. Add diced onion and garlic to bacon drippings in pan; sauté until onion is soft. Add diced ham, and heat thoroughly. Add parsley, basil, and tarragon; toss together. Add white wine; bring to a simmer. Add reserved bacon, season with white pepper, and cook over medium heat for 5 minutes. Stir in bread crumbs and remove from heat.

Coat baking sheet large enough to hold the six trout with oil. Divide stuffing equally among each trout, placing in cavity. Fold fish to close cavity and place on baking sheet; place 1 pat of butter on top of each fish. Bake in 375 degree oven for 10 to 12 minutes. Serve one whole fish to each guest, drizzling any remaining liquid in pan over each fish.

WHITE RIVER TROUT FRY

Submitted by: Virgil Ward

Clean trout, leaving on the head. Roll in lemon-lime soda batter, salt to taste; place in large iron skillet with plenty of cooking oil. Fry until golden brown.

OZARK SUCKER FRY

Submitted by: Corey Cottrell

Prepare fish by scaling. Fillet or gut the fish.

Scoring fish: Slice straight down (through tiny bones) as close together as possible. On filleted fish, score from the meat side down to the skin side. Be careful - don't slice all the way through.

Place fish in yellow cornmeal and shake in container to cover fish completely. Heat frying grease or peanut oil to temperature that when you place fish in, they bubble instantly. Cook until the fish are floating and when you squeeze with tongs they seem crispy, not mushy. Place on paper towel to drain.

VANCE'S BAKED WHITE BASS

Submitted by: Randy Vance

Pat dry 6 to 8 white bass fillets (from fish of 1 to 2 pounds each).

Roll in saltine cracker crumbs, salt and pepper. Lay fillets in 9x13 glass baking dish. Drizzle with mixture of ½ cup creamy Caesar's dressing and ¼ cup fine Chardonnay or Sauvignon Blanc. Bake at 400 degrees for 30 minutes or until flesh flakes with fork.

Serves nicely with saffron rice, fresh French cut green beans and French bread.

Serves 4.

RACK OF WALLEYE

Submitted by: Keith Kavajecz

This is an easy recipe to use for cooking fish on a grill. It can be used with any fish fillets from the size of a 2-pound walleye up to a 20-pound lake trout. The nice aspect of this recipe is that it will cook out some of the fat of the fish and therefore some of the fishy taste. One of the important factors with any fish recipe is to prepare the fillets before cooking by removing stomach fat and any blood lines. Especially on the skin side of the fillet there will be a dark strip of fat. By removing this your fish will not be as "fishy" tasting.

3-5	pounds of fish fillets	1 teaspoon garlic salt
1	stick butter or margarine	

Run the grill on high for 5 minutes before cooking. Put the fillets between wire racks like those used for cooling bread. These racks are inexpensive or you can purchase wire racks made for cooking on the grill with a handle attached. Turn the grill down to low. Place the rack of fish on the grill and cover - cook for 5 minutes. Melt the butter with the garlic salt, making garlic butter. Brush on uncooked side of fish. Flip racks using pot holders and brush garlic butter on cooked side of fillets. Cover and cook for 5 minutes. Brush garlic butter on top side and flip. Cook for 3 minutes. Brush garlic butter on top side and flip. Cook for final 3 minutes or until fish flakes apart.

Note: Cooking times may vary based on the temperature of grill. DO NOT OVERCOOK FISH. Dried out fish will taste fishy. With thin fillets you may only have to cook it for the first 2 five-minute periods. Once the fish is done, it can easily be taken off the racks and still maintain its nice fillet shape.

"*Rare indeed is the sportsman who, squatted on a gravel bar or huddled under a rain-drenched tree, can whip up a meal that resembles anything other than last week's garbage.*"
—Joel Vance, "Confessions of an Outdoor Maladroit"

Stream of Life

Sit on a streambank
And watch it flow by
It calms the hurts, and heals the heart,
Yet, I know not why.

Use your eyes and see the water
Drift away in a daydream.
Sorrows and worries will fade,
Such are the powers of a stream.

Fish finning in the current,
Oblivious to human strife.
They swim, feed, and reproduce.
All, without the stress of human life.

Learn all you can from the stream,
With all its beauty and grace.
Perhaps you then can improve
Upon the plight of the human race.

Remain strong and fluid, my friend,
Just like the stream.
God will provide direction
If you simply dream.

—Bill Cooper

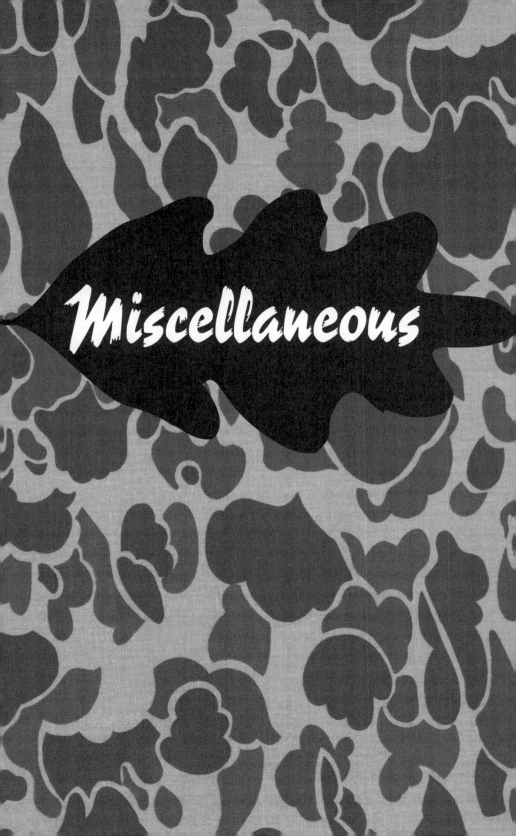

Miscellaneous

> *"The only thing better than being outdoors at dusk is being there with good people, a cold drink and the mingled aromas of driftwood smoke and a well-tended Dutch oven tickling your olfactory lobe. At moments like this, it's hard not to fancy yourself an oriental potentate."*
>
> —Jim Low
>
> Big Piney River float trip,
> Missouri Outdoor Communicators, 1998

BIG PINEY RIVER FLOAT TRIP

STRAWBERRIES ROMANOFF

Submitted by: Hank Reifeiss

¼	cup sugar	2	tablespoons sugar
¼	cup Grand Marnier	2	tablespoons Grand Marnier
4	cups whole strawberries, cleaned and sliced in half		Pinch of cinnamon
1	cup whipped topping	½	cup sour cream

Combine ¼ cup sugar and ¼ cup Grand Marnier in a bowl; stir until sugar dissolves. Add strawberries. Toss gently and place in zip lock bag. Refrigerate until ready to use. Add 2 tablespoons sugar, 2 tablespoons Grand Marnier and cinnamon to whipped topping. Fold in sour cream until smooth. Spoon cream mixture in bottom of serving glass. Top with strawberries and repeat.

Author's Note: This was "the favorite" recipe on the 1998 Missouri Outdoor Communicators Big Piney Float!

APPETIZERS

Submitted by: Spencer Turner

20	finger-size pieces breast meat of woodcock, quail, duck, doves, pheasant, chukkar, goose or any combination	1	cup extra virgin olive oil Greek seasoning
		6-8	slices bacon

Dip each meat piece in olive oil, sprinkle each side with Greek Seasoning and place on plate. Marinate overnight or up to 3 days in refrigerator. Remove from refrigerator and wrap each piece with a small piece of bacon. Secure with toothpick. Broil until tip of toothpick begins to char; turn and repeat broiling. Takes about 2 to 3 minutes per side. Do not overcook. Serve warm right from the oven.

Legs can also be used and I have served this appetizer with homemade hot/ sweet mustard dip.

APPLE FOR DESSERT
Submitted by: Bob Whitehead

Before leaving home for a camp out, mix cinnamon and sugar in plastic, air-tight container. At the campfire, prepare a hot-dog stick. Peel apple and place on pointed end of stick. Heat the apple over the campfire. Periodically roll in cinnamon and sugar and heat over campfire, slicing and eating glazed apple as you continue to cook over the fire.

BAKED BEANS
Submitted by: Bob Whitehead

It is a "pet peeve" of mine to see someone open a can of "so-called" baked beans and heat and serve. Take a little time spicing up your beans and you will enjoy them much more.

Brown about a pound of ground beef or pork sausage with garlic salt and onion; I like jalapeño peppers in mine. Add this to two cans of baked beans (one can of baked beans and one can of red beans works great). Add a teaspoon of rosemary, a teaspoon of thyme and a half cup of brown sugar. Heat and serve.

CLARIFIED BUTTER
Submitted by: Kate Fiduccia

Clarified butter is the "pure" butter that is left once the mild solids have been separated out. It is not as hard to achieve as you might think. Simply take a 1 pound block of butter and melt it in a small saucepan over low heat. Skim off the white foam from the top. The clear or clarified butter will be in the middle and the milk solids will be at the bottom. To keep clarified butter handy, you can melt two or three pounds at once, ladle out the clarified butter and keep it in the refrigerator to melt and use for future recipes.

CAJUN POTATOES

Submitted by: Boomer Sutton

4-5	potatoes, cut coarsely	1	jumbo onion
1-1½	smoked sausages		Hot sauce
	Mushrooms		Salt and pepper

Wrap in foil and put on grill 45 to 60 minutes.

CAMPFIRE POTATOES AND ONIONS IN FOIL

Submitted by: Jared Billings

Lay out a large sheet of heavy-duty aluminum foil. Wash a large potato and slice into quarters. Slice quarters into pieces. Do not peel potato. Place pieces in center of foil. Peel one small or ½ medium onion. Dice into large pieces. Add to potatoes in center of foil. Add ⅛ stick of butter or margarine. Season to taste with salt and pepper. Seasoned salt may be substituted for table salt. Chili powder may be substituted for black pepper. Carefully wrap potatoes and onions by lifting the longer edges of the foil upwards and folding downwards several times creating a seal. Fold up the ends of the foil in the same manner, creating a seal. It is important to use a large enough piece of foil.

Place the foil package in the coals of a campfire being careful not to puncture the foil. You may puncture the folded ends in order to use a fork or use tongs to handle package by the folded ends. Cook 20 to 30 minutes. Do not open until ready to serve. Be careful of escaping steam.

OZARK STYLE GRILLED CORN-ON-THE-COB

Submitted by: Jared Billings

Gather a roll of heavy-duty aluminum foil, sliced bacon and brown sugar. Lay out handy on kitchen counter.

Go to cornfield. Cut desired number of ears of corn and run back to the kitchen, shucking corn along the way. Or, you can use ears of corn not so fresh. Wrap a strip of bacon around each ear of shucked corn. Lay each ear on its own large piece of foil. Add a pinch of brown sugar to each ear. Carefully wrap the corn by lifting each of the two longer edges of foil upwards and folding the edges downwards several times creating a seal. Fold up the ends of foil in the same manner, creating a seal. It is important to use a large enough piece of foil.

Place on barbecue grill for 30 to 45 minutes. Do not open foil until ready to serve. Be careful of escaping steam.

CRAWFISH STEW

Submitted by: Kyle Hicks

¼	cup flour	1	teaspoon pepper
¼	cup butter or margarine		Hot sauce to taste
1	medium onion, finely chopped	1	pound peeled crawfish tails
¼	cup bell pepper, chopped	2	tablespoons chopped parsley
1	clove garlic, minced		
1	rib celery, finely chopped	2	tablespoons chopped green onions
1	teaspoon salt		

Sauté butter or margarine and flour until golden brown, stirring constantly. Add onion, bell pepper, garlic and celery. Cover and sauté for 5 minutes over low heat. Add ¾ cup water, salt, pepper and hot sauce. Simmer 1 hour. Stir in crawfish tails, cover and cook over low heat for 5 minutes. Uncover and cook until stew thickens. Add parsley and green onions just before serving. Serve over hot, fluffy rice.

CRUSTY GLAZE FOR BROILED FISH

Submitted by: Paul Hansen

⅓   **cup pecans or walnuts, finely chopped**
1-2   **tablespoons butter**
¼   **cup brown sugar (or ⅛ cup maple syrup)**

2-3   **fish fillets (any white fleshed fish - walleye or striped bass are particularly good)**

As the fillets are broiling, melt butter in heavy saucepan, add nuts. Gradually add brown sugar or maple syrup until mixture is a paste. (Not dry and not liquid). Just before serving, top fish with the crust (spread over entire surface of the fish), and return to broiler for just a minute. Watch carefully so mixture bubbles, but does not burn.

ELK DROPPINGS

Submitted by: Chad Schearer

2   **cups sugar**
½   **cup milk**
¼   **cup cocoa**
1   **stick butter or margarine**

1   **cup coconut**
3   **cups rolled oats, uncooked**

Place in saucepan: Sugar, milk, cocoa and margarine. Mix and bring to boil. Boil rapidly for one full minute.

Remove from heat and add coconut and rolled oats. Mix well and drop by teaspoonfuls on waxed paper or foil; let cool.

FISH
Submitted by: Cheryl McDonald

Wake up at 5:30 a.m.

Walk around swimming pool to boat dock.

Start engines; fish, fish, fish; catch large dolphin (mahi mahi, dorado).

Bring it back to the dock.

Fillet into thick steaks.

Marinate in beer.

Spark up the grill.

Grill lightly on each side until fish is soft and flaky.

GRAMMA SCHEARER'S FISH BATTER
Submitted by: Chad Schearer

1	cup flour
½	cup milk
2	eggs
2	tablespoons shortening
1	teaspoon baking powder
1½	teaspoons salt

Mix together and coat fish. Fry fish in deep fryer until golden brown.

Cooking Bannock

Bannock has long been a traditional woodsman's bread. It is made by simply baking biscuit dough in a floured skillet on the windward side of the fire. Turn the loaf over when done on one side, and both sides will be ready in about fifteen minutes. Coals shoveled out and put behind the pan quicken the baking of the under side.

David Besenger © 1998

ELSIE'S FISH SAUCE

Submitted by: Casey Iwai

1	cup soy sauce	4	slices fresh gingerroot
½	cup mirin or sherry	2	cloves garlic
½	cup water	½	cup sugar or less, to taste

Combine ingredients and allow to develop full flavor in refrigerator overnight. Will keep for weeks. Can be used with any firm-fleshed white fish fillets that are coated with flour and pan fried over medium heat, turning once when golden. Usually 5 to 7 minutes per side depending on thickness. Heat fish sauce, adding fresh green onion as it is heating. Pour sauce over cooked fillets. Serve at once with sauce, steamed white rice and pickled vegetables.

Elsie was Casey's paternal grandmother who died before he was born. She was an exceptional cook who did wonders with Asian foods.

WILD GAME DIP

Submitted by: Jim Strelec

1	can tomatoes with diced chiles	1	pound ground venison, elk or caribou, browned
1	pound processed cheese loaf, cut in cubes		

Mix all ingredients in crockpot until cheese is melted. Stir occasionally. Serve hot with chips.

"One of the most noble acts an outdoorsman can do is to take a child hunting or fishing so they, too, can enjoy the great outdoors."

—Bill Jordan

SHRIMP GUMBO

Submitted by: Kyle Hicks

1	cup baked roux	1	large onion, chopped
	Salt, red pepper, black pepper to taste	2	pounds shrimp, prepared for cooking
1	tablespoon parsley, minced		Water
	Gumbo filé, optional	2	tablespoons onion tops, chopped

Select a large, deep pot because gumbo likes to boil over. Place the roux in the pot along with the chopped onion. Heat slowly and sauté the onion only until wilted. Add about 8 cups cold tap water and season generously with salt, black and red pepper. Bring to a boil. Reduce to medium and cook for an hour, stirring every now and then to keep the roux from clinging to the sides of the pot.

Add the shrimp which have been cleaned and deveined and cook for 20 minutes. If juice has cooked down too much and seems too thick, add a cup or two of HOT water.

Add onion tops and parsley and cook for 10 more minutes. Taste for seasoning and add more if necessary. Turn off heat. Cover pot with lid and allow it to set for 15 minutes. When ready to serve, heat the gumbo until hot but do not boil. Ladle into gumbo bowls over rice which has been cooked in separate pot. The bottle of gumbo filé should be placed on the table for those wishing to add a teaspoon or less to their serving. It is a unique spice that also serves as a thickening ingredient.

HUSHPUPPIES

Submitted by: Tim Huffman

1	box corn muffin mix	Pimentos and/or green peppers (optional)
	Milk	
	Onion	

Follow instructions on box, except use less milk. Let sit unstirred for at least 10 minutes. The mixture will rise and thicken. Drop by teaspoonfuls into hot grease. Cook until golden brown. Drain on paper towels.

HOT SWEET MUSTARD

Submitted by: Spencer Turner

1	cup dry mustard	2	eggs, beaten
1	cup balsamic vinegar	1	cup firmly-packed brown
5	cloves garlic		sugar

Combine mustard, vinegar and garlic. Let stand overnight. Combine mixture, eggs and brown sugar in top of double boiler. Cook 20 to 25 minutes; longer cooking time will produce more dense mustard. Spoon into sterilized jars.

Mustard can be served with just about anything. I've used it with salmon, ham, deer, sweet bologna and even with quail and woodcock.

ITALIAN EGGS

Submitted by: Mark Van Patten

6	jumbo eggs	½	cup Parmesan cheese
1	cup Italian marinara sauce	½	cup Romano cheese
		¼	cup milk
½	cup rehydrated porcine mushrooms	¼	teaspoon salt
		½	cup sliced black olives
¼	cup prosciutto (Italian ham) sliced very thin and chopped		Fresh ground black pepper to taste
			Olive oil

Get olive oil hot, almost to the smoking point. Drop in prosciutto and frizzle until crisp. Drain on paper towel and set aside. Lower heat and wait for oil to cool, then scramble 6 eggs in olive oil. Add all ingredients (except the cheeses) when they are done. Divide into equal portions for 4 persons. Sprinkle Parmesan and Romano cheeses on top of servings. Garnish with parsley sprig and serve.

MARINADE FOR VENISON

Submitted by: David Blanton

1¾	pounds venison roast	½	cup water
2	lemons, juiced	¼	teaspoon seasoned pepper
1	cup wine vinegar	¼	teaspoon seasoned salt
2	medium onions, thinly sliced	½	cup ketchup
2	stalks of celery with leaves, chopped	1	clove of garlic, minced
1	teaspoon chili powder	2	bay leaves

Combine all of the ingredients. Place the venison roast in a glass casserole dish with lid. Pour the marinade over the venison roast and cover. Turn every 12 hours for at least 12 to 24 hours.

Marinade may be used to baste the roast when cooking.

MOREL AND EGGS

Submitted by: Ron Kruger

Fresh morel mushrooms, if you can find them, are the finest delicacy in the outdoors.

Clean mushrooms and soak in saltwater overnight. Cut into small pieces, dredge in flour and sauté in butter. Beat eggs. Add salt and pepper to taste. Pour eggs over mushrooms and cook to desired consistency.

OUTSTANDING ONION

Submitted by: Ray Eye

1	whole Vidalia onion	3-5	bacon strips
2	beef bouillon cubes		

Peel off outer layer of onion. Use a sharp, pointed kitchen knife to core the onion from one end. Do not core completely through the onion. Be careful to save a plug from the core you removed.

Place two beef bouillon cubes inside onion and close the onion with the core plug. Completely wrap the onion with uncooked bacon strips. It may be helpful to hold the bacon strips in place with toothpicks.

Wrap the onion in heavy-duty aluminum foil and place directly on hot coals of your smoker or barbecue pit. Open occasionally and test with fork until onion is cooked to desired tenderness.

It is best to wait until bouillon cubes are dissolved and have seeped into the onion juices.

PUMPKIN SOUP

Submitted by: Paul Hansen

1	cup chicken stock	¼	teaspoon cumin
2	cups pumpkin (canned or cooked and mashed)	1	jalapeño pepper or scotch bonnet (optional)
¼	cup minced onion		Garnish with sour cream
2	tablespoons celery		or plain yogurt and
½	teaspoon oregano		chopped cilantro
½	teaspoon rosemary		

Sauté onion and celery with spices. Add to stock and pumpkin in saucepan. Simmer for flavors to mingle. If using hot pepper, cut it in half lengthwise, and simmer in soup. Take it out before serving or puréeing. If smooth consistency is desired, pour all (except pepper) into blender and purée. Serve hot. Optional ingredients are minced garlic and grated fresh ginger. A treat is to place a scoop of pumpkin soup in a bowl alongside a scoop of black bean soup. Swirl together, garnish and serve.

OZARK RED BEANS AND RICE

Submitted by: Mark Van Patten

	Rice (to serve 4)	1	teaspoon fennel seeds
2	beef bouillon cubes	1	can red beans
¼	teaspoon salt	1	pound pork sausage
	Cayenne pepper to taste	1	can tomatoes with chiles
	Black pepper to taste		(drained)

Brown sausage and drain. Set aside. Bring water to boil for rice. Add salt, pepper, cayenne pepper, bouillon cubes, fennel seeds and rice. When rice is ready to remove from heat, add red beans and sausage. Stir and cover. Leave covered long enough for the red beans and sausage to warm, then serve.

This dish makes a great main course. Serve it with hot, home made bread with plenty of sweet butter and corn on the cob. A slice of fresh apple pie and a dollop of vanilla ice cream for dessert is a nice finish.

BAKED ROUX

Submitted by: Kyle Hicks

4	cups flour	2	cups cooking oil

Select a thick pot, such as a Dutch oven. Mix the flour and oil together. Place in oven and bake at 375 degrees for 1½ to 2 hours, stirring about every fifteen minutes so it will brown evenly. Should be a rich brown when done. When cool, it can be stored in the refrigerator for future use. Will keep indefinitely.

BLACKENED REDFISH

Submitted by: Will Primos

1	tablespoon dried, minced onion	4	tablespoons butter or margarine, melted
1½	teaspoons cayenne	1	tablespoon peanut oil
½	teaspoon each: garlic powder, celery salt, dried thyme, and salt	4	redfish fillets (about 6 ounces each), patted dry
¼	teaspoon pepper		

This recipe for blackening seasoning can be used on many types of fish. Be sure to open your kitchen windows and turn on your stove fan while grilling this recipe.

Combine onion, cayenne, garlic powder, dried thyme, celery salt, salt, and pepper. Mix butter and peanut oil with blackening spices. Place blackening mixture into a shallow bowl. Roll each fish in the blackening mixture. Set fish on a plate and refrigerate until ready to grill.

Preheat stove top grill. Cook fish over high heat for about 2 minutes. Make sure your kitchen is well ventilated; open a window. Turn fish over, cover with the grill lid, and continue cooking over medium-high heat for 2 to 3 minutes longer or until fish is cooked. Fish will blacken slightly on the outside and be opaque on the inside. Remove to serving plate.

SWEET, SWEET POTATO

Submitted by: Bob Whitehead

Wrap sweet potato in foil. Bake over campfire. Open potato and sprinkle with cinnamon. Add butter. Delightful!!

SCOTT'S POTATOES

Submitted by: Scott Bennett

5	pounds red potatoes, quartered		Hot pepper
8	pieces of processed cheese loaf		Seasoned salt
¼	stick of butter	1	Cavender's Seasoning piece of plastic wrap, 4 feet long

Boil quartered red potatoes adding seasoned salt, hot pepper and Cavender's Seasoning to water before you bring to a boil. Boil red potatoes with the skin on to add to the flavor. Once potatoes are done, use a colander to run off excess water and replace potatoes in pan immediately. Add butter and cheese on top of potatoes as well as more hot pepper if you want the potatoes to be real spicy. Cover pot with plastic wrap using the long piece to totally seal in all heat (which will make butter and cheese melt down perfectly). Once this has been done (3 minutes) uncover and serve. This is very easy to make and has been a huge hit every time I serve it. It also goes great with any wild dish.

SHRIMP CREOLE

Submitted by: Kyle Hicks

2	pounds shrimp, cleaned and deveined	1	large bell pepper
2	cups onions, chopped	4	pods garlic, minced
1	cup celery, chopped	1½	teaspoons sugar
1	(6 ounce) can tomato paste	1	cup green onion tops, minced
2	(6 ounce) cans tomato sauce	1	cup parsley, minced

Season shrimp and set aside. Sauté onions and celery in butter. Add tomato paste, tomato sauce and four cups of water. Cook one hour, stirring occasionally. (Add water if sauce becomes too thick.) Add the shrimp and the other ingredients. Cook over low heat for 30 minutes. Serve over steamed rice.

TERIYAKI GLAZE

Submitted by: Casey Iwai

⅔	cup soy sauce	½	teaspoon minced fresh
½	cup brown sugar		gingerroot
¼	teaspoon monosodium glutamate	1	teaspoon (heaping) corn starch
¼	cup sake (rice wine)		

Mix ingredients. Heat in microwave (approximately 1 minute at 80% power) or heat on stove until mixture thickens. Spread glaze on fish (or on poultry, meat). Cook on barbecue grill.

WALDO'S FAVORITE MARINADE

Submitted by: Paul Hansen

3	parts soy sauce	Plenty of minced garlic
1	part red wine	and fresh, coarse ground pepper

Equal amount of Worcestershire sauce as wine.
Adjust amounts to taste.

Use to marinate steaks of any kind, chunks of venison or beef for kabobs or as a jerky marinade.

For jerky, cut strips of meat into thin slices, marinate for several hours or overnight in the refrigerator; place strips on cookie sheets in single layer; bake in oven on low temperature (about 200 to 250 degrees) for 3 or 4 hours. Time depends on how dry you prefer the meat. Check occasionally. Should be fairly dry but chewy, to very dry. Dryer is better for camping where refrigeration is not possible. Store long term in plastic bags in freezer.

THE POT-HERB THAT SAILED WITH THE PILGRIMS

THE POT-HERB THAT SAILED
WITH THE PILGRIMS

The Pilgrims landed in Massachusetts, and slowly made farms for themselves as they cleared the forest. They had a hard time at first, but the Indians helped them; sometimes with gifts of venison, and sometimes by showing them plants in the woods good to eat.

There was a squaw named Monapini, "the Root-Digger," who was clever at finding forest foods. She became friendly with a white woman named Ruth Pilgrim. Ruth learned much from the squaw and provided her family lots of wild edibles from the woods.

One day, long after the cleared farms were doing well, the white woman said, "See, Mother Monapini, thou hast shown me many things, now I have somewhat to show thee. There hath grown up in our wheat field a small herb that must have come from England with the wheat, for hitherto I have not seen it elsewhere. We call it lamb's-quarter, for the lamb doth eat it by choice. Or maybe because we do eat it with a quarter of lamb. Nevertheless it maketh a good pot-herb when boiled."

The old Indian woman's eyes were fixed on the new plant that was good to eat: and she said, "Is it very good, oh white sister?"

"Yes, and our medicine men do say that it driveth out the poison that maketh itch and spots on the skin." After a moment Monapini said, "It looketh to me like the foot of a wild goose."

"Well found," chuckled Ruth, "for sometimes our people do call it by that very name."

"That tells me different," said the Indian.

"What mean you?" said Ruth.

"Is not a goose foot very strong, so it never catcheth cold in the icy water?"

"Yes."

"And this hath the shape of a goose foot?"

"Yes."

"Then my Shaman tells that it is by such likeness that the Great Spirit showeth the goose foot plant to be charged with the driving out of colds."

"It may be so," said the white woman, "but this I know. It is very good and helpeth the whole body."

The Indian picked a handful of the pot-herbs, then stared hard at the last; a very tall and strong one.

"What hast thou now, Monapini?" The red woman pointed to the stem of the lamb's-quarter, whereon were long red streaks, and said: "This I see, that, even as the white-man's herb came over the sea and was harmless and clean while it was weak, but grew strong and possessed this field, then was streaked to midheight with blood, so also shall they be who brought it-streaked at last to the very waist with blood - not the white men's but the dark purple blood of the Indian. This the voices tell me is in the coming years, that this is what we shall get again for helping you-destruction in return for kindness. Mine inner eyes have seen it." She threw down the new pot-herb and glided away, to be seen no more in the settlements of the white man.

So the Indian woman read the truth in the little pot-herb that sailed and landed with the Pilgrims. And the lamb's-quarter still stands tall in our fields to this day, streaked with the remembrance of the blood of a passing race.

WHITE SAUCE FOR FISH

Submitted by: Rick Olson

½	cup plain yogurt	½	teaspoon dill weed
½	cup sour cream	¼	teaspoon dry mustard
¼	cup mayonnaise	¼	cup chopped onion, optional
2	teaspoons lemon juice		
2	tablespoons tartar sauce	1	clove chopped garlic, optional
1	teaspoon lemon pepper		

Blend together very well. Pour over about 1½ to 2 pounds of white fish (Walleye, crappie, etc.) Top with cheddar cheese and dried onions. Heavily butter a shallow baking dish. Bake in 350 degree oven 30 to 40 minutes. (Microwave 15 to 20 minutes, until fish is flaky).

Optional: Place onion and garlic on top of fish before the sauce.

WOO'S FAVORITE CORNBREAD

Submitted by: Woo Daves

2	eggs	⅔	cup cooking oil
1	cup grated sharp cheddar cheese	1½	cups self-rising corn meal
1	cup buttermilk	2-3	chopped jalapeño peppers
1	(8 ounce) can creamed corn		

Blend eggs, buttermilk, oil and peppers. Add the corn, cheese and corn meal. Stir till all ingredients are mixed well. Grease an iron skillet, heat until smoking. Add cornbread mixture and bake at 375 degrees for 1 hour.

> *"A hunter's world may be small in geography, but still be complete. A watchful squirrel hunter who spends fall days in the same woodlot each year can learn more of the wild world than the unobservant fellow who fills a trophy room from the ends of the earth under others' guidance, but who has seen little besides his targets."*
>
> —Charles F. Waterman

Small Game

BARBECUED BEAVER IN APPLE JUICE

Submitted by: J. Wayne Fears

Apple juice   **Salt and pepper**
Meat from one beaver **Barbecue sauce**

Clean and dress animal. Soak cut up meat in apple juice overnight. Drain. Cover meat with barbecue sauce. Place in oven at 350 degrees for one hour or until tender.

Cooperative Extension Service, Mississippi State University

BAR-B-Q BEAVER

Submitted by: Ralph Duren

Skin and dress beaver, discard rib cage. Cut off all fat and gristle, especially over the hindquarters. Make sure to remove the castor glands and the oil glands from underneath the tail on both sides of the vent. Cut off the tail and feet and discard. Save the glands for lure making.

Pre-boil the remaining large pieces of meat with pepper and onion until tender (usually 3 to 4 hours). Chunk up and remove from the water and bake in oven at 250 degrees until brown. Then add a generous amount of BBQ sauce. Bake until well done. Beaver come in various sizes due to their age. The kits of the year average 15 to 25 pounds. They are the best and the most tender. The older beaver (two years old, 35 to 45 pounds and older 50 to 80 pounds) will need to be pre-boiled longer to be tender. When fully cooked, the meat should fall off the bone.

FRIED BEAVER

Submitted by: J. Wayne Fears

Cut beaver into serving pieces and marinate overnight in salt water with 2 bay leaves and 4 cloves. Roll in seasoned flour and brown in butter and bacon drippings. Add small amount of water, cover pan, and cook until tender.

BAR-B-CUE RACCOON

Submitted by: Bill Cooper

Remove the kernels (brown glands located between the muscles in the neck and tail under the legs and along the flanks). Some are removed with the skin. These produce a strong, offensive flavor if not removed. Quarter the raccoon and remove as much fat as possible. Soak the raccoon in salt water overnight. Afterwards, parboil the raccoon in a solution of:

1	cup vinegar	**Use enough water to**
4	onions	**cover the meat. Parboil**
4	apples, quartered	**until tender, then strip**
	Bottom part of stalk of	**meat from the bones.**
	celery (no leaves)	

Sauce:

2	sticks butter (or one cup of oil)	2	tablespoons Worcestershire sauce
1	cup of vinegar (or lemon juice)	2	tablespoon dry mustard
½	pound brown sugar	1	tablespoon black pepper
			Salt to taste

Warm sauce in pan. Stir well. Use it to baste the raccoon, as it slowly cooks in 225 degree oven for 2 to 2½ hours. Do not rush it. Slow cooking lets the flavor of the sauce sink in.

SQUIRREL ON RICE

Submitted by: Bill Cooper

3	squirrels, cut up	½	teaspoon salt
1	cup of your favorite BBQ sauce	½	teaspoon pepper
		1	small onion

Boil squirrels with small onion until meat easily comes off bone. Place meat in sauce pan. Sprinkle with salt and pepper. Cover with BBQ sauce. Simmer slowly for 20 minutes. Serve over rice.

Serves 4.

113

OZARK STYLE BARBECUED WILD TURKEY
Submitted by: Jared Billings

Remove tendons from breast meat. Bluntly divide into four large pieces. Using a very sharp knife, slice each breast piece across the grain making several steaks about ¾-inch thick.

Place steaks in a large, flat dish. Cover them with the entire contents of a large bottle of Italian salad dressing (vinegar and oil, not creamy). Marinate in the refrigerator for two to four hours, making sure all surfaces of the meat are in contact with the dressing.

Remove meat from marinade and allow excess to drip from the pieces. Save the marinade. Add a healthy dose (to taste) of Liquid Smoke and the juice from ½ of a lemon to the left over marinade.

Optional: Wrap each piece of meat with a strip of bacon and secure with toothpicks as you would a filet mignon.

Place meat on grill over charcoal or gas fire. Using a brush, immediately begin basting each piece with marinade, turning frequently. Do not allow flames to flare up and burn the meat. Continue until marinade is used up or for 30 minutes. Reduce heat. Using a brush, begin basting with your favorite tomato-based barbecue sauce, continuing to turn frequently and not allowing flames to flare up and burn the meat. Continue basting and turning for another 30 to 45 minutes until done to taste. Do not simmer meat in sauce at any time.

Serve hot with fresh-baked cornbread, Bob Whitehead's baked beans, wilted watercress (or lettuce) salad and cold beer. Breathe deeply and sigh.

"A peculiar virtue in wildlife ethics is that the hunter has no gallery to applaud or disapprove his conduct. Whatever his acts, they are dictated by his own conscience, rather than onlookers. It is difficult to exaggerate the importance of this fact."

—Aldo Leopold

BASIC BEAVER MEAT PREPARATION

Submitted by: J. Wayne Fears

Clean and dress the beaver. Cut the beaver into chunks. Prepare baking soda solution using 2 tablespoons of baking soda per gallon of water. Boil meat in solution for 5 minutes.

With dull knife, scrape away and discard fat. Though there won't be much fat, this is an important step. Cut into bite-size pieces and salt to taste. Cook in pressure cooker for 20 minutes at 10 pounds pressure; discard water. Debone meat. Meat is now ready for use in stews, soups, simmered in barbecue sauce or treated as beef in any recipe. I still use Buck Rievers' fried beaver recipe and find it quick and easy.

ATLANTA SPECIAL

Submitted by: J. Wayne Fears

While I was working with an outfitter in the Chugach Mountains of Alaska, I learned how to cook beaver with a delicious recipe called Atlanta Special.

1	beaver (8 to 10 pounds)	Celery leaves, if desired
1	bay leaf	Flour
2	medium onions	Fat
1-2	garlic cloves	Salt and pepper

Remove nearly all fat from beaver. Cut up as you do rabbit. Soak overnight in salt water.

Parboil until about half-cooked in water with the bay leaves, onions and garlic. Celery may be added, if desired. Drain, roll in flour and brown in hot fat and season with salt and pepper. Bake in covered pan in a moderate oven until tender. Gravy may be made from the drippings. Plan the same number of servings as from a similar weight of pork.

BEAVER TAIL
Submitted by: J. Wayne Fears

Beaver tail was once a favorite food of pioneers. Strung on a cord and worn around the waist or slung over the pommel or a saddle, beaver tails kept many a mountain man fed on the trail. Today, there are very few outdoorsmen who can say they have tried this backcountry delicacy. As Horace Kephart put it in his writings early in the 1900's: "This tidbit of old-time trappers will be tasted by few of our generation, more's the pity."

The meat of the beaver tail is tender, white and gelatinous. Roast beaver tail is quick and easy to prepare. Simply place the unskinned tail on a campfire grill or charcoal grill until the scaly black skin puffs and flakes. Turn over and heat the other side. Then this can be easily skinned off. Season the tail to taste and eat. If you are using the thick tails of older beavers, first boil them until tender, then place on the grill.

Roast beaver tail may be cut up into small pieces and boiled with a pot of beans as you would pork. It makes a pot of beans very tasty.

BEAVER FAJITAS
Submitted by: Corey Cottrell

A true hillbilly meal. Beaver is very lean and tastes a little like beef. The meat from one large beaver (35 pounds) will feed 2 to 3 adults. Beaver fajitas are made just like any other fajita.

1	tomato, diced	Sour cream
	Lettuce	Picante sauce
8-10	large flour tortillas	Cheese

Meat used on fajitas is the tenderloins along with bits and pieces of meat off the hams. Take the meat and cut it into small strips approximately 3 inches long and 1 inch wide. Place the meat into a frying pan or electric skillet. Cover meat and simmer for 15 to 20 minutes, occasionally stirring. Add spices or tenderizer to your liking. After the meat is cooked, mix and match vegetables and additives to your liking.

CAJUN RABBIT

Submitted by: Stacey King

3-4	pounds meat	½	teaspoon oregano
1	large onion, cut up	1	tablespoon parsley
½	large green pepper, cut up	3	tablespoons ketchup
1-2	stalks celery, cut up	¾	teaspoon cayenne (or to taste)
2	cloves garlic, cut up	1	cup cider
2	tablespoons oil		

In Dutch oven, brown meat in oil with onion, green pepper, celery, and garlic. In small mixing bowl, blend oregano, parsley, ketchup, cayenne and cider and pour over browned rabbit. Cover and bake in 350 degree oven for 4 to 5 hours. Serve over rice.

CHICKEN SANDWICH SPREAD

Submitted by: Kevin Howard

Kevin's mother has been fooling people for years with her "Chicken" Sandwich Spread. It's delicious as a sandwich filling or served on crackers.

1½	cups chopped rabbit	⅓	can cream of chicken soup
¼	cup chopped pickles		
	Soda crackers	¼	teaspoon celery salt
1	teaspoon Worcestershire sauce		Salad dressing

After boiling the rabbit, take meat off bone and put through a food grinder with pickles and soda crackers to clean out grinder occasionally. Add remaining ingredients and enough salad dressing to moisten filling and give the spread the desired consistency.

ROAST BEAVER

Submitted by: J. Wayne Fears

Soak beaver overnight in ¼ cup vinegar and water to cover. Wash in cold water, place in roaster. Cut several slits in meat. Sprinkle with salt and pepper. Put strips of fresh salt pork over slits and dust with a little flour. Add about ¼ cup water to the pan and roast with lid on until half done. Add more water, if needed.

Cut up enough onions, celery and carrots to fill 1 cup. Sprinkle over meat. Finish roasting uncovered. Beaver should be cooked until meat falls off bones. Make gravy by adding flour and water to juices and vegetables in the pan.

TRADITIONAL COTTONTAIL

Submitted by: Mike Roux

Once you have butchered the rabbit, soak it in cold salt water for a couple of hours. This will help remove any clotted blood that may be present from either a wound from the shot or from field dressing. Drain the water and allow the pieces to dry. Lightly sprinkle the rabbit with your favorite seasoning salt and place in a pressure cooker for seven to ten minutes. While it's being tenderized, mix two cups of flour with a tablespoon of salt, a tablespoon of pepper and a teaspoon of garlic powder.

When the rabbit comes out of the pressure cooker it will be hot and wet. Carefully place the pieces, one at a time, in the flour mixture and cover the meat. Place the pieces in a skillet with hot olive oil and fry until a golden brown crust appears. Use the trimmings left in the pan to make milk gravy; add biscuits, corn on the cob and a salad and you're set.

This is the traditional fried rabbit meal that I've had since childhood.

HOT RABBIT
Submitted by: Bill Cooper

2	rabbits, cut into serving portions	½	teaspoon salt
1	cup smoke-flavored barbecue sauce	½	teaspoon pepper
		2	teaspoons hot sauce

Boil pieces for 30 minutes. Drain. Place pieces in deep pan. Salt and pepper. Mix hot sauce with BBQ sauce. Cover pieces with sauce. Simmer for 30 minutes.

Serves 4.

RABBIT CASSEROLE
Submitted by: Brad Harris

Cook rabbit in slow cooker until meat easily removes from the bone. Debone rabbit and lightly brown in skillet. Put large can of mixed vegetables or your own combination of veggies in casserole dish. Add rabbit. Mix 1 can of chicken soup, 1 can of cream of mushroom soup and 1 can of milk. Salt and pepper. Pour mixture on top of vegetables and meat. Bake 1 or 2 cans of biscuits and separate and place on top of mixture. Cover and place in oven at 300 degrees for 30 minutes. Uncover and cook additional 10 minutes.

SMOKED BEAVER

Submitted by: J. Wayne Fears

My favorite method of cooking beaver, when it's my time to cook in camp, is to smoke the critter in a charcoal water smoker. These ingenious smokers are very popular and are sold at hardware stores, camping supply houses, etc. I start out by marinating the beaver pieces overnight in a marinade made of 1 cup of vinegar, 2 cups of cooking oil, 2 tablespoons pepper, 1 tablespoon garlic salt and 1 tablespoon of Worcestershire sauce.

Next, I put the marinade in the water pan of the smoker and place a handful of green hickory chips, mesquite chips or apple wood chips (depending on what is available), on the hot charcoal. I place the beaver meat in the smoker and allow it to smoke for 7 hours. When served with slaw and baked beans, it is always a camp favorite.

SQUIRREL OR RABBIT
WITH GARLIC & TOMATOES
(a.k.a. Dead Eye's Delight)

Submitted by: Nick Muckerman

1	squirrel or rabbit, cut up		Dash Worcestershire
2	tablespoons olive oil		sauce
1	tablespoon chopped	1	teaspoon dried basil
	garlic	¼	teaspoon dried rosemary
1	(14 ounce) can chopped	¼	teaspoon salt
	tomatoes	¼	teaspoon pepper

Heat stainless steel skillet over medium-high heat. Sear meat pieces in preheated dry skillet, turning once, until lightly browned and crispy. Reduce heat to medium-low. Add olive oil and stir. Add garlic and stir for 1 minute. Add tomatoes and remaining ingredients; stir well to incorporate. Cover and simmer for 20 minutes. Serve with crusty garlic bread and romaine lettuce salad.

TREE RAT (SQUIRREL) AND DUMPLINGS
Submitted by: Brenda Valentine

Kill (head shoot if possible), skin and clean 2 to 4 squirrels. Pick off any stray hairs you may have allowed to get on the meat. Soak in cool salt water for a couple of hours or overnight to draw the blood. Boil gently in a large pot with a small chopped onion, two pinches of salt, and a generous dash of black pepper. A pod of red pepper works real well, also. Cover the pot and continue cooking at a gentle boil until the squirrel meat loosens from the bone. Remove the squirrels and drop the dumplings into the still simmering broth. Pull meat from the bones and return to the pot. Cook for about 15 more minutes, but do not stir vigorously.

Dumplings

Stir together until blended into a soft dough: 1½ or 2 cups of plain flour and a healthy pinch of salt. Moisten with broth from the cooked squirrels. Drop by the teaspoonful or roll out on floured wax paper and cut into strips.

BEAVER TAIL SOUP
Submitted by: J. Wayne Fears

2	beaver tails		Vinegar
	Salt		Pepper
1	bay leaf	2	cloves garlic, minced
3	carrots, sliced	3	stalks celery
2	small onions	2	cups egg noodles
1	small can peas, drained		

Skin and remove all fat from tails of 2 beavers. Cut up tails in small pieces and soak overnight in water with 2 cups of vinegar and 2 tablespoons salt for each quart.

Place meat in kettle with 4 quarts of boiling water. Add ¼ teaspoon pepper, 1½ teaspoon salt, bay leaf, garlic, carrots, celery and onions. When meat is almost tender add egg noodles and peas.

121

POT HOOKS

Keep several pot hooks of varying lengths available to permit choosing one to suspend your food the proper height above the fire.

The gib is made by splicing two sticks together. Hooks on the two sticks should face each other. One hook can be used to hold the kettle, and the other will hook over the lug pole. A nail or lashing will hold the two sticks together.

A pot hook has a notch cut in it that slants downward and is deep enough to hold a kettle handle securely.

Wire pot hooks are made of heavy material which will not straighten under weight.

A gallows crook is made by leaving a strip of tough bark extending from one end of a stick. The bark is bent into a loop and locked to the stick to make a handle. The lug pole must be slipped through the loop making the gallows crook very stable.

The hake uses a large nail for a kettle hanger. The wooden hook hangs over the lug pole.

—Bill Cooper

"*I hunt for the pleasure, but much of the pleasure is in eating the birds and other game I shoot. There are many reasons: Game is largely devoid of contamination; it is leaner and thus better for my body; properly prepared, game tastes far better than the sterile, bland meat raised under production-line conditions. A game dinner should be a ceremony, both of eating and as a resolution to the hunt.*"

—Joel Vance, "Bobs, Brush and Brittanies"

POT HOOKS

BAKED BEAVER WITH SWEET POTATOES

Submitted by: J. Wayne Fears

Another method of cooking beaver I learned, while working at a wild turkey hunting camp, is baked beaver with sweet potatoes. This excellent recipe was the creation of Dr. Lewis Shelton, Extension Wildlife Specialist at Mississippi State University.

1	dressed beaver, halved		Sweet potatoes
2	pounds fatback, rinsed free of salt	10	large onions
		4	pounds oleo
¼	cup black pepper	½	cup salt
8	medium-sized hot, green peppers	2	cups red cooking wine

Boil all of the above ingredients except oleo, sweet potatoes and beaver, for 15 minutes in ½ gallon water. Place each beaver half in large baking pan. Remove fatback and pour boiled ingredients equally over beaver halves. Add 1 gallon water to each pan. Spread 2 pounds of oleo over each half of beaver.

Slice fatback and divide equally over each half of beaver. Bake at 350 degrees for 7 hours or until tender.

Boil sweet potatoes, removing peel after they are tender. Place cooked potatoes around each cooked beaver half and continue baking for 30 minutes. If pan is too crowded, remove beaver before baking potatoes in sauce. Be certain potatoes are covered with sufficient sauce and butter.

To serve, remove meat from bones and place on serving tray with potatoes arranged around the meat.

Upland Game

SAYING GOODBYE TO THE McGUFFIN

SAYING GOODBYE TO THE MCGUFFIN

I called him McGuffin. I stole the name from Alfred Hitchcock. The suspense movie director always had a gimmick, the thing that everyone was after, and he called that "the McGuffin."

McGuffin du Calembour was a French Brittany and between the moment I met him on an airline loading dock at St. Louis Lambert airport until I laid him in a rocky grave on the hill across the lake, he was my best friend.

It was a dozen years-plus. McGuffin didn't recognize the advances of age. Age was for old dogs; Guff was the eternal puppy. Every day was the best day he ever had. He yawped against the kennel fence every time anyone opened the house door, sure it meant a trip to some bird field.

Guff was an eternal optimist. He could be cold and wet, covered with snow, pelted by sleet, even struck down by heat exhaustion, but those were minor inconveniences, all part of being there. And being there was life.

Something poisoned Guff. One day he was healthy, the next he was ill and the third day I was burying him, sobbing disconsolately. I still can't visit the grave without breaking down. Maybe never will.

I took him to the far slope, across the lake where the afternoon sun slants through the oak trees and lights and forest floor.

Nearby is an old log, covered with moss, that I found one day years ago. It looked like a good place to sit and think. I've gone to this log often. Sometimes I'm pretending to squirrel hunt; other times it's turkeys or deer, but mostly it's just thinking...or sometimes not even that, just soaking in the feel and smell of the earth and the sky.

It's a sweet place and I took McGuffin there knowing it made no difference to him whether the sun warmed his grave or not. It just makes a difference to me. I wanted him to be where I have felt content.

There's a new puppy, but he will not be McGuffin. The puppy is only a successor, not a replacement. He will carve his initials on my heart just as Guff did.

He and I will share times of glory and times of ignominy through the years, just as Guff and I did. Probably I'll grow to cherish him as much as I cherished Guff. I know that...but I miss my old friend so much.

Animal rights advocates and I seldom agree, yet when they lobby for the term "animal companion" instead of "pet," I can see the point. Guff was my friend more than my dog.

I was never lonely on long trips when he was with me. He listened to me shoot off my mouth and he always sensed when I was blue. He was the only one of the dogs who enjoyed being hugged and who would tuck his soft face under my arm and comfort me with his warm presence.

I can't estimate how many miles we traveled together. It was many thousands, to states as far away as Idaho. He pointed ruffed grouse in the bogs of Minnesota and pheasants in the Dakotas.

But it was Missouri quail that we both cherished. Guff pointed his first quail at just over five months in an old field in north Missouri. It was a sunny November day, typically warm for early season. He was chuffing the air as if chewing the scent out of it.

His eyes were squinted and he trembled with intensity. I shot the bird and he found it dead in the foxtail and I was inordinately proud of my little dog.

Guff wasn't a pretty pointing dog. No calendar artist would have picked him. But when he was on birds, as opposed to rabbits or possums or various other wildlife that he also enjoyed hunting, there was no doubt.

I remember him tiptoeing through a bog that reeked of woodcock scent. He walked on eggs, soaking wet from vegetation and a misting rain, but he didn't care. He was surrounded by game birds and all else was immaterial. Finally, he locked on point, and I walked the bird up and shot it.

Guff stood by it. Wouldn't pick it up. He didn't much like to retrieve. He'd rather find a downed bird and make sure I saw where it was, then move on to new games.

Another time, we relaxed against a log with a pair of grouse atop it. He'd pointed both and I, with rare skill, had killed them. I ate a cold apple and gave him a chunk. The thin sun lit the fallen leaves. I knuckled his ears and stroked him gently, knowing that such moments must be cherished because they are bound to end.

I'd intended to take Guff dove hunting the day he got sick. But it was hot and I went fishing instead and never got to have that last hunt with my friend. His first hunt was for doves. He was nine weeks old and fell asleep on my shell vest, rousing only a bit when the gun went off. He sniffed the dead birds with puppy delight, then went back to sleep.

Guff was more than a hunting dog. He rode a canoe like the lookout on the Santa Maria, ever eager for the sight of something other than water. In his old age, he took up fishing.

He'd lie on the dock, his feet over the edge, and watch the circling blue-gills below, trembling so violently he was a blur. Jimmy Houston never got that excited about fishing. If I hooked a catfish, he'd wade in as I led it to shore and offer to help land it.

It's always intrigued me that hunters, who make mistakes routinely (like missing more shots than they hit) expect perfection from their dogs. Guff never came close to perfection.

He was just an intelligent and skilled bird dog with an average nose, but sometimes he screwed up almost as badly as I did. There was a memorable day when Guff did absolutely everything wrong. First, he busted birds. He acted as if he couldn't have smelled them if they'd been glued to his muzzle. Then he rolled in a cowpie. I got him reasonably cleaned up and brought him inside the cabin at the hunt's end.

He promptly threw up. While I was cleaning up that mess, yelling at him, he pouted over to the duffel bag of a fellow hunter and flopped down on it...depressing the nozzle of a can of WD-40 inside. The entire can emptied inside the bag.

Guff never turned down a dogfight and never won one. He was covered with scars. His eartips, lacerated by a decade's-worth of briars, were scarred and often bled after a tough day in the field. He had several scars on his face from losing encounters with his grandson, Dacques.

Dacques hero-worshiped Guff for a couple of seasons, followed him everywhere. Then, with young dog arrogance, Dacques decided he was the heir-apparent and Guff was over the hill. He was wrong, of course, but you can't tell a young dog anything.

Guff had been the same way. After a first season when he made few mistakes, he hit the sophomore jinx. He knew it all. It took another year of hard work and often impatient instruction before he settled back down. Once he realized it was a partnership between him and me, we melded like solder and a metal joint.

Dacques became a better bird finder. He has a great nose and good range, more like a pointer than a Brittany. I loved to hunt with him. But when I wanted a day by myself, more to get away than to kill birds, I'd load Guff and we'd take our time working the fields and draws and creek edges.

I knew he'd find some birds and hold them forever. I didn't have to worry about where he was because we each always knew where the other was. It was like a marriage. We merged personalities and became as one. Guff and I, a couple of old dogs, scarred and stiff and comfortable with each other.

That's why I feel as if I've lost a piece of me.

So, from time to time, I'll go to the mossy log and sit there and think about McGuffin and me. There needs to be an end to mourning and there are those who will say it's silly emotion even to cry after dead dogs. The new pup will warm the cold spots in my heart. It took a long time to get over the death of Guff's predecessor, but I did.

Life moves on and dead dogs don't come back.

They just leave great dark holes in the November landscape where once they flamed like the sun.

—Joel Vance

WOODCOCK À LA TURNER

Submitted by: Spencer Turner

½-¾ cup uncooked wild rice
     Water
1   teaspoon chicken
     bouillon granules
1   onion, coarsely chopped
½   cup butter
     (not margarine)
2-3 cloves garlic, chopped
1-2 woodcock, separated into
     legs and breasts
     (When I have time, I fillet
     the meat off the breast
     bone)

1   tablespoon poultry
     seasoning
     Salt and black pepper to
     taste
2   cups cream sherry
     (not cooking sherry)
     Fresh mushrooms, sliced
1   (10 ounce) can cream of
     mushroom soup,
     undiluted

Cook wild rice by placing in a 2-quart cooking pan, adding water to three-fourths full. Add bouillon. Bring to a boil, reduce heat and simmer until rice has puffed to about triple original size and tender. Drain and set aside. Sauté onion in butter until clear. Add garlic and woodcock seasoned with poultry seasoning, salt and black pepper. Sauté over medium heat about 10 minutes, turning breasts and legs until lightly cooked. Add sherry and mushrooms and simmer covered for another 10 minutes. Add soup and mix. Combine woodcock with wild rice and bake in oven at 325 degrees for 20 to 30 minutes. I usually serve this with stir-fried, gingered baby peas and shrimp, hot garlic bread and a tossed salad, and a bottle of good German Riesling wine.

COOKING BAG QUAIL

Submitted by: Joel Vance

Skin six quail and cut out backbone, strip innards, then cut birds in half. For a marinade, mix ½ cup dry white wine, ⅓ cup olive oil, five drops sesame oil, 1¾ tablespoons fresh lemon juice, 1 tablespoon parsley, 1 tablespoon thyme, fresh ground black pepper to taste.

Marinate birds in a cooking bag for three or four hours, then bake at 250 degrees in the marinade for 1 to 1½ hours, testing for doneness. Serve with vegetable of choice.

Fruity birds: Mix 12 ounces of canned apricots, 2 tablespoons white wine, 1 teaspoon tarragon, 1 teaspoon dill, 1 clove garlic. Blend well in blender. Spread mixture over four to six quail or two grouse breasts (or pheasant) in baking dish. Bake covered at 250 degrees for 1 to 1½ hours.

OVEN BARBECUED QUAIL

Submitted by: Bill Jordan

Quail	**Bacon**
Salt	**Spicy barbecue sauce**

Wash quail, rub inside with salt. Place each quail on a square of foil. Pour 2 tablespoons barbecue sauce on quail breast. Lay ½ strip bacon across breast. Use butchers fold to close foil. Seal sides. Place packages of quail on cookie sheet. Bake at 325 degrees until tender, about 1 to 1½ hours.

BAKED CHUKKAR BREASTS

Submitted by: Charlene Cooper

2	tablespoons olive oil	¼	teaspoon black pepper
2	large cloves of garlic, minced	4	chukkar (or pheasant) breasts
	Grated peel and juice of one lemon	¼	cup chicken broth
½	teaspoon salt	2	tablespoons butter

Heat small skillet over medium heat. Add olive oil. When oil is hot, add garlic and sauté 30 seconds. Stir in lemon juice, salt and pepper and bring to a boil. Set aside.

Arrange chukkar in lightly buttered shallow baking dish just large enough to hold chukkar in single layer. Sprinkle with lemon peel. Cover with foil. Bake at 400 degrees for 30 minutes. Remove foil and bake and additional 30 minutes or until chukkar is cooked through. Transfer chukkar to 4 individual dinner plates and keep warm.

Pour liquid from baking dish into small skillet. Add chicken broth and bring to boil. Cook until reduced by about half and the mixture is syrupy. Gradually whisk in butter. Pour sauce over chukkar and serve immediately.

"There's really nothing to acquiring a good bird dog. All you need is a whip and a chair. That takes care of your wife. Now, about the dog."

—Joel Vance, "Confessions of an Outdoor Maladroit"

DEEP-FRIED TURKEY FILLETS
Submitted by: Shirley Grenoble

When we think of preparing wild turkey, roasting comes to mind. But since I found this recipe, it has become my favorite way to cook wild turkey. I haven't roasted a turkey in years.

Skin the turkey as soon after harvesting as possible. Fillet out each side of the breast. Freeze the legs for later use in soup or on the barbecue grill. Put the breast meat in the freezer long enough to firm it. When chilled and firm, slice the breast into pieces about ½-inch thick. Slice crosswise to the grain.

Salt each fillet strip and marinate for a while in an egg and milk mixture. Then batter with your favorite coating: flour, cornmeal, bread crumbs, or whatever you prefer, and drop into hot shortening. Be careful to not overcook.

"Among the woodland perils, the forked stick is the most diabolic. You trudge through the brush, bone tired and looking forward to a hot bath and bed, when it catches your foot in its crotch, the long end digs into the ground and begins to pivot, and momentum carries you forward with your foot trapped somewhere behind you, waving frantically on that devilish pivot point.
You are going ass over teakettle, no doubt about it."
—Joel Vance, "Bobs, Brush and Brittanies"

CAJUN DEEP-FRIED WILD TURKEY

Submitted by: Rob Keck

1	(10-15 pound) wild turkey	1	stick butter or margarine
5	gallons peanut oil	½	teaspoon garlic powder
2	tablespoons Cajun seasoning	½	teaspoon cayenne pepper (optional)

Pour peanut oil into a 10-gallon pot. Place pot on propane fish cooker burner and heat oil to 375 degrees. Dry turkey thoroughly. Tie two cotton strings around the carcass so bird can easily be lifted out of oil. Carefully submerge turkey in oil. Deep fry for 3½ to 4½ minutes per pound and cook until turkey floats to the top. Remove bird from oil, and immediately dust heavily with Cajun seasoning. Melt butter or margarine, and add garlic powder and cayenne, if desired. Allow turkey to cool slightly before carving. Brush with seasoned butter, if desired.

Yield: 12 to 16 servings.

QUAIL BREAST AND LEGS

Submitted by: Spencer Turner

Buttermilk	Garlic salt to taste
All-purpose flour	Butter-flavored vegetable
Salt and pepper to taste	oil

Dredge quail in buttermilk; then dredge in flour seasoned with salt, pepper and garlic salt. Fry in oil in cast-iron skillet until golden brown, turning once. Don't overcook.

CHUKKAR PARMESAN

Submitted by: Mark Van Patten

1	teaspoon rosemary	½	package onion soup mix
¼	cup sun-dried tomatoes (chopped coarsely)	2	chicken bouillon cubes
1	cup fresh Parmesan cheese (grated)	2	cups flour Olive oil Brown rice (enough for 4 servings)
¼	teaspoon salt		
¼	teaspoon black pepper (coarse)	4	chukkar breasts (quail or chicken will work as
¾	cup cream, or half and half		well)

Dredge chukkar breasts in flour thoroughly. Place flour in bag and add breasts. Shake until breasts are covered in flour. In large frying pan heat olive oil and get good and hot, almost but not quite to smoking. Place floured breasts in pan and brown on all sides. After browning, lower heat and cover. Allow ample time for breasts to cook slowly and become tender. Remember to turn occasionally. Remove from oil and drain on paper towel when tender.

NOTE: If your birds are older and tough, you may need to pressure cook them after they are browned to tenderize.

Put chopped sun-dried tomatoes, rosemary, salt, pepper and bouillon cubes in water for rice. Bring water to a boil and add rice. Cook rice according to directions. After rice is done, stir and fluff to distribute rosemary and tomatoes throughout evenly. Set rice aside.

When preparing any sauce, make sure that everything else is set aside. You need to devote all of your attention to the sauce. The sauce needs constant stirring to be smooth and creamy. It is essential to the success of any dish that the sauce be perfect.

In a sauté pan on low heat, blend cream, onion soup mix and half of the Parmesan cheese. Stir constantly until mixture is smooth and cheese is melted into the sauce. Salt to taste. If you want pepper, use white pepper. If the sauce is to thick, thin slightly with water. If your sauce is to thin, prepare cooled flour rue and add to thicken. (With rue, it is always better to add cold to hot or hot to cold to eliminate lumps). Serve chukkar breasts over a bed of rice.

DOVE BREASTS MARINATED AND SAUTÉED IN MERLOT

Submitted by: Randy Vance

Use four doves per person. Pluck out the breast, then fillet by pushing thumbs against the breastbone, slide thumbs between meat and breast bone to peel out the breast meat. Lay breasts on shallow dish and pour one cup fine Merlot over breasts. Cover and set aside for one hour.

30 minutes before serving, bread dove breast in flour. Using about one tablespoon of olive oil per two breasts, sauté minced garlic, ginger and chopped green onions together until onions are bright green. Lay in dove breasts, add salt and pepper, then brown in oil, turn when ready.

After breasts are browned on both sides, pour remaining Merlot marinade in pan, cover and simmer about 15 to 20 minutes until breasts are done. If marinade has cooked down too much to pour over all servings, add water and reconstitute sauce remaining in pan.

Lay breasts over bed of rice or mixture of wild and white rice. Pour sauce over breasts and rice. Great served with portobello mushrooms and snow peas on the side.

GRILLED DOVE

Submitted by: Mike Pearce

Fillet meat from breast (possibly marinate in soy or teriyaki sauce). Wrap each breast in ½ piece of bacon, fasten with toothpick. Alternate serving suggestions: 1-inch slices of duck, goose or turkey (these meats need marinade). Try a chunk of pineapple in center of meat. jalapeño peppers work well with long strips of duck, goose or turkey. Cook on grill until done.

GRILLED DOVE BREAST

Submitted by: Tom Evans

| 12 | doves | 1 | tablespoon pepper |
| 1 | tablespoon salt | 12 | slices bacon |

If you have more doves, use half slices of bacon. This marinade will cover several.

Marinade

1	small bottle Worcester-shire sauce	2	cups oil
1	small bottle steak sauce	2	tablespoons chili powder
1	chili pepper, chopped	1	(9-ounce) jar of prepared mustard
4	cloves garlic, chopped	1	tablespoon salt
2	cups margarine	1	tablespoon pepper
1	tablespoon hot sauce		

Marinade should be mixed and simmered for one hour. Rub doves with salt and pepper; wrap with bacon slice, secure with toothpick. In large bowl, put doves and cover with marinade and refrigerate overnight. Place birds on grill over medium heat and cook until tender - usually about 15 minutes. Baste and turn often. Garnish with lime juice.

EAT QUAIL FRESH FROM THE FIELD

Submitted by: Charlie Farmer

Skin quail and remove entrails. Rinse with water. Place on ice in a cooler. In electric skillet set at 200 degrees, sauté whole quail to light brown in canola oil. For 12 or more quail, use two, 10 ounce cans of cream of mushroom soup. Mix with one can water. Stir and pour over quail. Pepper to taste. Salt lightly. Cover and cook for one hour at 200 degrees until done. Do not overcook. Serve with rice, biscuits and vegetables.

RUNNING GEAR DRESSING

Submitted by: Steve Stoltz

1	drumstick (from wild turkey)	1	tablespoon of chicken bouillon
1	thigh	¼	cup of chopped onion
1	(6 ounce) box of chicken flavor stuffing mix		

Fill large sauce pan ¾ full of water. Add chopped onion and chicken bouillon to water and bring to rapid boil. Add drumstick and thigh to boiling water. Boil for approximately 40 minutes. While meat is boiling cook stuffing. Drain meat and let cool. De-bone all meat and dice in small pieces. Add diced meat to stuffing and mix meat with stuffing. (If mixture is too dry, add ½ cup water at this point). Pour stuffing from sauce pan into a medium size baking pan. Spread stuffing evenly in pan and cover with foil or lid. Bake stuffing for 45 minutes at 325 degrees. Uncover and bake another 10 minutes for crisp topping.

This is a great way to cook the dark meat on a wild turkey. This can be served with gravy and biscuits as a meal or it goes great with fried or baked wild turkey breast!

GARLIC PHEASANT

Submitted by: Jim Strelec

2	pheasants, cut up	Salt and pepper
	Oregano	Butter or margarine
	Italian seasoning	Garlic salt

Place pheasant pieces in baking dish and sprinkle each with spices listed above. Put a pat of butter on top of each and broil in 500 degree oven until browned; takes just a few minutes. Remove from oven and turn pheasant pieces and put spices on the other side, also adding a small pat of butter or margarine to each. Place back into 500 degree oven and brown. When both sides are browned, turn oven down to 350 degrees and bake until fork tender; approximately 40 to 50 minutes.

GRAVELBAR FAJITAS

Submitted by: Hank Reifeiss

½	cup vegetable oil	¼	teaspoon cumin
½	cup lime juice	6	skinless, boneless turkey breast halves
¼	cup red wine vinegar		
¼	cup finely chopped onion	1	avocado
4	garlic cloves, finely chopped	1	red pepper
			Green onions
1	teaspoon sugar		Salsa and hot sauce
1	teaspoon oregano	8	8-inch flour tortillas
½	teaspoon salt		

Combine oil, lime juice, vinegar, onion, garlic, sugar and spices in zip lock bag. Add turkey breasts, turning to coat each side. Keep refrigerated. Slice peppers in half and clean. Clean green onions. Wrap tortillas in foil and warm on side of grill. Lightly oil peppers and onions and grill. Chop peppers and onions. Wrap in foil and keep warm. Remove turkey from marinade. Grill until done. Slice turkey in thin strips. Wrap turkey, vegetables, chopped avocado, salsa and hot sauce in warm tortillas.

Makes 6 servings.

NOTE: Chicken breasts work well for this recipe also.

GRILLED TURKEY BREAST

Submitted by: Alex Rutledge

1	stick butter	Lemon pepper, to taste
½	sliced turkey breast, ½-inch thick	Garlic salt, to taste
		Dale's seasoning, to taste

Get grill very hot. Season meat with ingredients. Cook meat to preference. Brush meat with butter and Dale's seasoning every time meat is turned. I like to turn meat every 2 minutes.

ITALIAN FRIED TURKEY BREAST

Submitted by: Eddie Salter

1 turkey breast cut in 2 to 3-inch strips Italian dressing Salt and pepper	Buttermilk Eggs Flour

Marinate cut up breast in Italian dressing at least 1 hour, longer if possible. Break 1 to 2 eggs, according to amount of breast, in a bowl. Add ½ to 1 cup of buttermilk to egg mixture. Pour marinade off breast, salt and pepper. Drop breast pieces in buttermilk and roll in flour. Deep fry until a light brown.

PHEASANT MY WAY

Submitted by: Chris Kirby

Debone four whole pheasants, cutting into strips roughly one inch wide and ½-inch thick. Clean and place in bowl. Using an oil and vinegar based Italian dressing, completely cover the pheasant. Completely cover pheasant with grated Romano cheese. Add season salt, pepper, and garlic salt to taste.

Let pheasant marinate for 15 to 30 minutes. Place marinated pheasant in large skillet, making sure there is extra dressing in the skillet that will boil and sink into the pheasant. Cook on medium/high heat. Continue to stir and turn pheasant chunks until a golden or brown crust develops on the outside edges of pheasant. Serve with chicken flavored rice.

PASTA GOBBLER

Submitted by: Tad Brown

2	pounds wild turkey breast cut into thin strips	1	cup cooked spaghetti Oyster sauce Soy sauce
1	cup celery, diced		Vegetable oil
1	cup fresh mushrooms, chopped		Corn starch
1	cup fresh bean sprouts	1	chicken bouillon cube
1	cup yellow onion cut into ½-inch rings	1	cup water Garlic powder
1	cup broccoli florets	1	teaspoon red pepper flakes

Marinate turkey, pepper flakes, 1 tablespoon of oil, 2 tablespoons of oyster sauce and 2 tablespoons soy sauce in dish for 1 hour. Dissolve bouillon in water, add 2 tablespoons oyster sauce and 2 tablespoons soy sauce. Set aside. Heat 2 tablespoons oil on high heat in wok or large non-stick pan. Coat meat mixture with 2 tablespoons corn starch and stir fry for a few minutes until no longer pink. Remove meat. Add more oil if needed and stir fry onion, celery and broccoli until tender crisp, add mushrooms, bean sprouts and cook 2 more minutes. Add pasta and meat and mix well. Add bouillon mixture and toss until thickened. Remove from heat and serve immediately plain or over rice.

WILD TURKEY NOODLE SOUP

Submitted by: Steve Puppe

2	turkey drumsticks	3	celery stalks sliced to ¼-inch
2	turkey wings		
1	pound frozen egg noodles	1	small onion sliced, if desired
3	carrots sliced to ¼-inch		

Boil drumsticks and wings until meat is tender. It may need to be picked off the bone. Save desired amount of water to fill 5 quart kettle, when other ingredients are added. Cook until vegetables and noodles are done.

PHEASANT WITH ARTICHOKE HEARTS

Submitted by: Jim Dougherty

Unbleached, whole wheat pastry or barley flour can be used for the white sauce and the seasoned flour in this recipe.

1	2 to 3 pound pheasant, skinned and cut up	1	(9 ounce) package frozen artichoke hearts
	Seasoned flour	2	tablespoons flour
3	tablespoons oil	2	tablespoons butter
⅓	cup sliced green onions	1	cup chicken broth
1	cup sliced fresh mushrooms	½	cup dry white wine

Dredge pheasant pieces in seasoned flour. Heat oil in heavy skillet and brown pheasant pieces on all sides. Remove to baking dish with a cover. Sprinkle with mushrooms, green onions and artichokes. Pour ¼ cup of chicken broth in casserole; cover tightly and bake at 350 degrees for 50 minutes.

Melt the 2 tablespoons butter, add flour, stirring, and add remaining chicken broth and wine. Cook till smooth, stirring constantly. Pour sauce over pheasant and reduce heat to 325 degrees. Bake uncovered another 25 to 30 minutes.

CHURCH SUPPER PHEASANT AND QUAIL

Submitted by: Ralph Duren

1	pheasant or 6 quail or combination of both	1	cup raw rice
		1	package onion soup mix
2	ribs celery, sliced	2	cups water
3	medium carrots, sliced	¼	cup margarine

Sauté pheasant and quail pieces in margarine and remove from pan. Sauté vegetables in same pan. Mix rice and onion soup mix together in bottom of a baking dish that has been greased. Arrange meat and vegetables on top of rice. Pour on water. Cover and bake at 350 degrees for 1 hour.

CATS AS RETRIEVERS?

Charlene and I shared a duck blind last fall with guide Bill Fletcher, in Hoxie, Arkansas. The rice fields were frozen, the skies were clear, and the ducks were not cooperating.

As hunters so often do, to enjoy their hunt together, even though the game doesn't cooperate, we began to tell stories.

The duck pit "story of the day award" went hands down to Bill Fletcher. Bill related about the fabulous dove hunting he used to enjoy near his home in Mountain Home, Arkansas. "Everybody knows how a dog hates to retrieve doves, because of the feathers," Bill quipped. "Well, I pretty much did without a retriever in the dove field, until my old cat began following us when we went dove hunting."

Bill went on, "I thought it pretty funny when the old cat went after the first dove I knocked down one afternoon. However, my laughter faded when the cat stopped halfway back with the dove, sat down and promptly ate it!"

"Not to give up on the possibility of having a dove retrieving cat, I gave it another chance," Bill told. "Darned, if that cat didn't eat the second dove, too! Thoughts of shooting the cat raced through my head, but that sure would have caused problems at home. Third time is a charm, right? Not in that cat's case. It ate my third bird, too!"

Bill Fletcher is a patient man. He has been guiding for stripers on Norfork Lake for 31 years, but a cat about did him in.

"Finally," Bill sighed, "that darned cat brought the fourth dove and dropped it at my feet. Soon the cat had a pile of doves that he guarded for me. My bad shooting buddies do sometimes try to even the odds by stealing some of my birds."

A cat retriever and bird guard both? Come on, Bill. "It gets better," Fletcher said, grinning like the cat that swallowed the canary. "One day me and a friend were dove hunting and the cat had retrieved all the birds we downed. Of course, the cat ate his usual three birds. That became the price we paid for its services. Anyway, my buddy feathered a dove. It didn't fall all the way to the ground, but didn't regain altitude either. The bird was flying about two feet off the ground straight at the cat's position. No lie, that cat jumped into the air, caught the flying dove in its mouth, did a backwards flip and landed on all four feet, and proudly added the bird to the pile!"

—Bill Cooper

BARBECUED QUAIL

Submitted by: Steve McCadams

6	quail, split in two	¼	cup water
¼	cup butter	½	teaspoon dry mustard
¼	cup onion, chopped	½	teaspoon salt
¼	cup green pepper, chopped	¼	cup dry, red wine

Sauté onion and green pepper in butter. Add rest of ingredients and simmer for 10 minutes. Place quail in piled, hinged grill and broil over very hot coals while basting with sauce for about 25 minutes. The quail may also be roasted in oven. Butter shallow baking dish and arrange quail, skin side up, in dish. Brush quail with barbecue sauce and roast in a preheated 450 degree oven for 25 minutes, basting once during cooking time with sauce. Serve with hot buttered rice.

Serves 3 or 4.

Note: Recipe from Sylvia Bashline's "Bounty of the Earth."

QUAIL IN CREAMY MUSHROOM SAUCE

Submitted by: Stacey King

2	(10¾ ounce) cans condensed cream of mushroom soup	5-6	quail, cut up
		2	tablespoons oil
		8	ounces fresh mushrooms, sliced
½	cup milk		
2	tablespoons sherry	1	medium onion, cut up
1	teaspoon salt	½	teaspoon dried thyme leaves
¼	teaspoon pepper		

In small mixing bowl, blend soup, milk, and sherry; set aside. In Dutch oven heat oil over medium-high heat. Add quail pieces; brown on all sides. Add onion, thyme and reserved soup mixture. Cover. Bake for 4 hours at 350 degrees. Add the mushrooms the last 30 minutes. Serve over rice or mashed potatoes.

You may substitute with two pheasants, cut up.

QUAIL IN PLUM PRESERVES

Submitted by: Karen Mehall

4-6	quail	Salt and pepper
1	jar plum preserves	Thyme
¼-½	cup margarine	

Clean quail and sprinkle with seasonings. Brown quail in margarine in frying pan. Turn down the heat, add several tablespoons of water as needed, and cover and cook until done. Sprinkle with more salt, pepper and thyme according to taste. Prior to serving, add plum preserves and cover until preserves are heated. Serve with drippings.

SMOTHERED QUAIL

Submitted by: Jim Casada

We first ate this dish when a delightful South Carolina Lowcountry couple, the Gregories, invited us to a weekend hunt at their place, The Bluff, where the movie "Forrest Gump" was filmed. Ann and Jane Gregorie created this recipe when they lacked some other desired ingredients. As is so often the case in cooking, improvisation produced fine eating.

6	quail	½	soup can sherry or to
¼	cup butter or margarine		taste
½	cup olive oil		
2	(10¾ ounce) cans chicken with rice soup		

Sauté quail in butter and oil, cooking to golden brown on all sides. Place in casserole. Pour soup and sherry into pan with drippings. Bring to a boil, stirring well to loosen brown bits. Pour sauce over quail. Bake, covered, at 350 degrees for 1 hour or until quail are tender. Serve with herbed rice, curried fruit and fresh asparagus. Six servings.

QUAIL WITH RASPBERRY VINEGAR

Submitted by: Will Primos

4	quail	⅓	cup raspberry vinegar
10	tablespoons unsalted butter, divided (all may not be needed)	½-1	cup chicken stock Fresh chopped tarragon for garnish
	Salt and pepper to taste		
1	tablespoon chopped shallots		

Remove backbone from quail and flatten, pressing down on breastbone. In a skillet, melt 3 tablespoons butter and brown birds on both sides. Season with salt and pepper and remove from pan. Add shallots to pan and deglaze with vinegar. Replace quail, add ½ cup stock, cover, and simmer until tender, 10 to 15 minutes. Remove quail. Either reduce liquid or add more stock to obtain ½ cup liquid. Bring to boil and whisk in butter, 1 tablespoon at a time, until desired consistency is attained. Adjust seasoning, add chopped tarragon, and serve over quail.

SPICY BACON DOVES

Submitted by: Eddie Salter

12-15 doves	Salt and pepper
12-15 slices of bacon strips	Jalapeño peppers
Italian dressing	

Preheat oven to 400 degrees or fire up the grill. Let bacon strips set at room temperature for about 30 minutes. Place doves in a bowl and marinate in Italian dressing for about 1 hour. Pour off marinade; salt and pepper doves. Take 1 jalapeño pepper and place against dove breast. Wrap bacon strip around dove and pepper; prick with a toothpick to hold. Repeat process with each dove. Place on grill or wrap in foil and bake in oven 30 to 45 minutes or until done.

SHAKE 'N' BAKE TURKEY
WITH RUNNING GEAR GRAVY

Submitted by: Rob Keck

This epicurean treat first hit the skillet back in the early 1950s by sheer accident when a tired and hungry turkey hunter was searching for a quick and easy evening meal at camp. Little did he know he was "greas'n the pan" of a craze which occurs regularly in a rural Pennsylvania county known as "Shake 'n' Bake" (not to be confused with the commercial variety). It has since been adapted to grouse, quail, ringneck and venison. As this granddaddy of turkey hunters and cookers stated at one of our spring hunt meals, "We've been living high on the hog, but this is on top of the world."

The bird should be skinned rather than plucked. White breast meat is filleted from the bone. Remove the one main tendon from the breast. Skinning and cut-up time is approximately 15 minutes. All appendages are disjointed. Cold-water soaking may be necessary if excessive blood appears. Breast fillets are cut across the grain about ¼-inch thick, 3 inches long and 1½ inches wide (about the size of a large oyster). When feeding a crowd, thinner and smaller pieces may be cut.

A mixture of 2 cups of milk and 3 beaten raw eggs is placed in a mixing bowl (more if needed). Into a second bowl pour ½ pound of bread crumbs (bread crumbs have proven superior over most other types of breading for this treat). A deep fryer or iron skillet may be used. Heat your oil to 365 degrees. Drop the turkey into the heated oil and turn it one time in the required 10 minutes. (When you drop any amount of cold meat into hot oil, it cools the oil; make sure the oil remains hot to set the breading. In the deep fryer I use 3 gallons of oil, so there is no significant cooling).

Extract the fried meat from the skillet or fryer, place it in a paper-towel-lined pan to soak up the excess grease and place in a warm oven until all is fried. A thick gravy is made from the neck, back giblets and legs and thighs. Most of the meat coming from the latter gives it the name "Running Gear Gravy" because that meat is cooked, browned, seasoned, cut up and added to the thickened broth. This gravy goes well on top of the fried meat, as well as potatoes or rice (a 15-pound bird easily feeds eight). Leftovers, if there are any, can be refrigerated after it cools, but you better put a lock on the refrigerator door!

SANDHILL CRANE

Submitted by: Dawn Charging

Requires at least six hours of prep-time after you have your destination.

1	four wheel drive vehicle	1	12 gauge shotgun
1	pair of Bushnell binoculars	1	box of BB or BBB steel shotgun shells
1	cell phone-to call for landowner permission		

Call your favorite hunting partner and drive to North Dakota.

This recipe requires good scouting the night before the hunt. Drive four-wheel-drive vehicle to hunting area. Sit on top of highest hill for best view, roughly 5 p.m. Use of good binoculars are a must for success with this hunting recipe. Scout area thoroughly. Watch exactly which field the crane uses to feed. Wait until sunset to insure that the flock stays in the same field until dark. This will insure they come back for breakfast at sunrise.

Fifteen minutes to sunrise, be sure all crane decoys are set. Canada goose decoys also work. Find good cover downwind of decoys. Make sure you are covered completely in camouflage, as these birds have incredible eyesight. Allow first flock to pass, allowing the flight line to pass over your decoys. Use good calling techniques and do not move until the moment of truth. Use good distance judgment as these birds often look closer than they are.

Enjoy a successful shoot and prepare for the real meal. Pat your partner on the back, yell, "Nice shot," a couple of times and retrieve your dinner. Upon arrival home, clean birds by pulling feathers away from the chest. Use a fisherman's fillet knife, cut the breast portions away from the bone. Next, cut away the legs for a caveman portion of drumsticks. Butterfly the breasts into 1-inch thick fillets. Marinate breasts and drumsticks in a mixture of water, dry onion soup mix and about 10 shakes of liquid teriyaki seasoning. Marinate for the rest of the afternoon.

Start your favorite gas or charcoal grill. Throw on a slow cooking grill; do not overcook. Be prepared for a juicy meal of red meat that doesn't "taste like chicken."

Eat meal, tell stories and repeat recipe for the following day.

STIR FRY PHEASANT

Submitted by: Keith Kavajecz

4	deboned pheasant breasts	8	ounces fresh mushrooms
1	bunch of broccoli	4	tablespoons soy sauce
½	white onion	1	tablespoon oriental sauce
4	carrots	½	tablespoon garlic salt
		½	cup baking soda

I use a small electric wok to cook in (any wok or electric frying pan will work). Because of the small cooking surface on an electric wok, the food must be heated in several steps to keep the vegetables crisp.

Cut breasts into 1x1x¼-inch pieces. Boil the bones in a quart of water to create a broth (or you can make broth with a bouillon cube). Peel outer layer off stem of broccoli and cut (stem and top) into ¼-inch strips. Cut onion into ¼-inch strips. Cut carrots and mushrooms into ¼-inch pieces

With the wok at high temperature:

Add half of the soy sauce, oil, and garlic salt to the meat in a small dish and let it marinate for 10 minutes to an hour. Coat the wok with a small amount of oil. Add broccoli and carrots. Stir and fry until the vegetables are warm, not cooked. Empty the wok into the wok cover. Add the remainder of the oil. Add meat and onions. Brown the meat; add oriental sauce and enough broth to cover the meat. Add broccoli, carrots and mushrooms. Stir together and cover for about 5 minutes. Stir and test flavor. Add more seasoning as desired. Cover and cook until broccoli is just getting tender, not soggy - 5 more minutes maximum. Mix baking soda with about a cup of water in a separate bowl. Slowly add this to thicken the broth in the wok while stirring. Serve with white rice.

Note: If you can cut the vegetables diagonally to expose more surface area it will enhance the taste.

HONEY SPICED TURKEY WITH ORANGE SAUCE

Submitted by: Ted Nugent

½	cup all purpose flour	1	medium onion, sliced
2	tablespoons vegetable oil	2	tablespoons cold water
3-3½	pounds of turkey, cut up or in 4 breast halves	2	tablespoons cornstarch
		1	cup orange juice
1	teaspoon salt	½	teaspoon ground ginger
1	teaspoon paprika	1	small (3½ ounce) can ripe olives
⅛	teaspoon pepper		

Dredge turkey in flour to cover all sides. In large skillet, heat oil; add turkey and cook over medium heat until brown on all sides, about 15 minutes. Place turkey in ungreased rectangular baking dish, 13x9x2 inches; sprinkle with salt, paprika and pepper; top with onions. Make a paste with water and cornstarch. Add orange juice, honey, lemon juice and ginger. Stir; pour over turkey, add olives. Cover and bake in 350 degree oven for 45 minutes. Garnish with parsley.

Serves 6 to 8.

TURKEY BREAST

Submitted by: Walter Parrott

1	deboned wild turkey breast
	Italian dressing with olive oil
	Worcestershire or teriyaki sauce

Slice breast across the grain into 2½ to 3 inch chunks. Place turkey breast in a zip-top plastic bag and marinate in Worcestershire or teriyaki sauce and Italian dressing for at least 2 hours. Grill until done. Do not overcook!

TERIYAKI PHEASANT STRIPS

Submitted by: Tom Evans

3	pounds of pheasant breast meat	½	cup good olive oil Coarse ground black pepper
1½	cups of teriyaki sauce		

Cut out all breast meat then cut into finger strips. Put pheasant strips in large bowl; add teriyaki sauce and hand mix to coat. Marinate overnight. Preheat oven to 400 degrees. Place strips on large oiled cookie sheet, slightly apart. Brush with remaining oil lightly coating each. Using pepper grinder, pepper to taste. Bake 20 minutes or until done (lightly browned). Do not over bake because they tend to become more like jerky. The jerky may be done also for a hunting treat, but be careful not to overcook.

WILD TURKEY BREAST

Submitted by: Corey Cottrell

1	whole turkey breast	4	cups flour
4	eggs		Salt and pepper
2	cups milk		Vegetable oil/peanut oil

Slice breast into chunks so they can be sliced again, which I call butterfly slices. Put these butterfly portions into the mixture of eggs and milk, which has been stirred. These portions can soak while you are butterflying or frying. After soaking portions, dip them into flour. Be sure whole portion is covered with flour. Put vegetable or peanut oil in skillet or deep fryer. Brown portions on both sides. Season to taste.

TURKEY CRISP

Submitted by: Brian Jenkins

1	egg	Lemon pepper
1	pound turkey meat	Flour
1	cup milk	Cooking oil
	Garlic salt	Pepper
½	teaspoon table salt	

Slice turkey off of bone ⅜-inch thick. Sprinkle lightly with garlic salt, lemon pepper and pepper, set aside. In large bowl, combine egg, milk and salt; mix well. Add flour until batter becomes creamy. Dip the turkey slices into the batter and drop into a large skillet with 1 inch of hot cooking oil. Fry until brown and crispy.

WILD TURKEY PARMESAN

Submitted by: Ralph Duren

1	egg, beaten	1½	cups spaghetti sauce
2	turkey breast cutlets	¼	cup grated Parmesan
	Salt	4	ounces mozzarella
3	tablespoons oil		cheese, shredded
	Pepper	⅓	cup bread crumbs

Combine salt, pepper, Parmesan, and bread crumbs. Dip turkey cutlets into egg, then coat well with bread crumb mixture. Brown on both sides in hot oil. Place in baking dish. Spoon sauce over cutlets and top with mozzarella. Bake at 350 degrees for 20 minutes or until tender. Serve with extra sauce and pasta on the side. Works best with young turkeys. May be adjusted for more portions.

TURKEY SALAD

Submitted by: Eddie Salter

3-4 cups cooked chopped
turkey (white or dark
meat)
4 boiled eggs, peeled and
chopped
Sweet relish

Mayonnaise
Mustard
Salt and pepper
½ cup cooked macaroni
(optional)

Combine all ingredients to taste. Serve with crackers or with lettuce and tomato.

WILD TURKEY SOUP

Submitted by: Larry Whiteley

1 turkey carcass
4-5 quarts water
4 medium carrots
1 small head cabbage
3 stalks celery
1 teaspoon salt
½ teaspoon pepper

½ teaspoon poultry seasoning
1 pound small macaroni,
precooked
Turkey gravy and
stuffing left over from
roast turkey dinner

Remove meat from the turkey bones; place the bones in an 8-quart pot and cover with water. Simmer for 2 hours or long enough to loosen the meat from the bones, but not long enough for bones to fall apart in the broth.

While the bones are simmering, grind all vegetables in a meat grinder. When the bones are done, set aside to cool. Add to the ground vegetables juice from vegetables and seasonings. Add any stuffing and remaining gravy. Simmer for about 2 hours. Clean remaining meat from bones and add it to the soup. When vegetable bits are tender and the broth tastes right, add cooked macaroni. Let stand for several hours before serving to allow the flavor to develop.

Serves 8 to 10.

GRILLED WILD TURKEY STRIPS

Submitted by: Steve Puppe

1	wild turkey breast cut into ½-inch strips	1	pound bacon
4	jalapeño peppers sliced to ⅛-inch		

Optional to marinate turkey strips in Italian dressing or Teriyaki sauce. Roll turkey strips around 3 to 4 pepper slices; wrap 1 slice of bacon around turkey, fasten with a toothpick. Grill over mesquite wood to desired tenderness.

These work great as an appetizer. Canadian goose also works well.

FRIED WILD TURKEY

Submitted by: Woo Daves

Cut wild turkey breast into bite-size chunks. Place in a pan, cover with milk and put 2 tablespoons of sugar and some garlic powder in the milk. Soak for 8 hours. Drain, roll in flour, salt and pepper the turkey. Fry until brown. Do not overcook. Delicious and mouth watering good!

> "A hunter's skills go far beyond finding and shooting game. He must know the habits and habitat of his quarry. He must exercise good workmanship skills by being able to recognize the various signs animals leave, then be able to conceal and position himself in a place that will give him the advantage necessary to harvest the animal."
>
> —Bill Jordan

GRILLED WOODCOCK BREAST

Submitted by: Bill Cooper

12	woodcock breasts	¼	teaspoon salt
6	slices bacon	¼	teaspoon pepper
2	cups Dale's Sauce		

Marinade woodcock breasts in Dale's Sauce 2 to 24 hours in refrigerator. Remove breasts from marinade. Sprinkle with salt and pepper. Wrap each breast with ½ slice of bacon. Secure with toothpick. Grill until bacon is done. Breasts are best slightly rare. Serves 4.

NOTE: Dove, snipe, quail or duck may be substituted.

WOODCOCK À LA NATURAL

Submitted by: Spencer Turner

This recipe came from Aldo Leopold's "Sand County Almanac." Although it takes some willpower to overcome the first-time germond's natural reluctance to eat birds with the entrail still inside, connoisseurs believe they are the best part of the bird.

1 or 2 woodcock per serving

Pick woodcock, removing head and feet. Do not draw or skin. I found that woodcock are best picked after cooling for 24 hours. The skin tears easily if picked warm. Place picked birds on baking sheet and bake at 500 degrees for 12 to 15 minutes. Do not overcook. Serve on wild rice.

A BOY BECOMES A HUNTER

A BOY BECOMES A HUNTER

In the eeriness of last Sunday's fog, I heard the boy yell, "Dove!"

I looked around in time to see him raise the 20 gauge and fire. Feathers flew and the bird cartwheeled into the corn stubble. Our chocolate lab, Mink, brought the dove to me before the last of the feathers, drifting in the damp air like a parachute, reached the ground. It was no easy shot, especially for a nine-year-old who last year struggled with the fear of pulling the trigger.

The little over-and-under gun did not quite fit him a year ago. Yet he begged me to let him try and I did. He had plenty of chances for doves and ducks. Scotty did everything right until it was time to pull the trigger. But for a little boy, he learned from target practice that the lightweight 20, an ideal youth gun, boomed like a cannon and punched like a boxer.

Last year, in the duck blind, a drake mallard seemed to take forever to cup closer into the decoys against a stiff wind. The boy was up and ready. The greenhead kept coming well within range and Scotty fought the challenge until tears welled in his eyes. He slid the safety back on and put the gun down. "I can't do it, Daddy, I just can't do it." And he burst into tears.

I told him not to worry. I thought it was a little early for him to start shotgunning anyway. And I mentioned that I was 13 before shooting my first shotgun. Next year he might be ready and there was no rush. The fact that he has hunted with me (without a gun) since he was five has been a great source of pleasure for us both. The boy looked up and wiped away the tears. He seemed to understand that there was much more to hunting than shooting. "I bet I'll be able to shoot next year," he told me.

Between then and now, Scotty grew taller and stronger. Our entire family took a 10-hour hunter education course in August. Regardless of age, or how many years a person has hunted, safety and ethics cannot be stressed enough. The course ignited our enthusiasm for the upcoming hunting season. A month ago he traveled to St. Louis with a friend and his family to witness a black powder, buck skinner rendezvous. He came back excited. "I shot a black powder pistol," he exulted. "It was loud and had a kick to it. But I did it. And there were kids there my age shooting black powder rifles. I think I'll be able to shoot Mommy's gun this year. When does dove season open?"

For the past few years, my wife Kathy could see the handwriting on the wall. She was about to lose her favorite shotgun.

The fog was reluctant to leave last Sunday. The doves that broke through the mist were on top of us before we knew it. Tricky shooting. The boy shot 15 times and killed two birds. My shooting percentage will not be divulged. I should have done better. Scotty did just fine. "I could hunt doves everyday," he proclaimed. "I can't wait for duck season." And the boy became a hunter.

—Charlie Farmer

"A man," I told myself when Brittany fever began to race through my system with the virulent passion of amoebic dysentery, "would have to be a fool to let himself in for the kind of humiliation I have seen bird dogs inflict on their suffering owners. I have watched the ears of my friends burn bright when their carefully trained bird dogs turned greyhound and vanished in pursuit of rabbits. I have seen their bragged-on dogs point possums and meadowlarks and catch and eat field mice with great gusto. I have seen their dogs chase cows while the farmer leaped up and down on the far slope, shaking his fist. I have watched their dogs roll ecstatically in fresh cow manure, then leap joyfully into their master's lap as the master prepared to enjoy a sandwich. I have seen their dogs either fight or make love all morning, while the rest of us waited patiently for them to hunt quail."

—Joel Vance, "Confessions of an Outdoor Maladroit"

Waterfowl

CROCKPOT DUCK

Submitted by: Bill Fletcher

2-3	duck breasts	3	medium potatoes
1	can mushroom soup	3	carrots
1	package dry onion soup mix		Mushrooms

Place duck breasts in crockpot. Add mushroom soup and onion soup mix. Fill with water to cover breasts. Cook on high for 2½ to 3 hours or on low for 5 to 6 hours. Add vegetables for last 1 to 1½ hours. Gravy is great on biscuits or mashed potatoes. This recipe will also work on goose, deer and squirrel.

DUCK AND WILD RICE CASSEROLE

Submitted by: Will Primos

2	medium ducks	½	cup red wine
1	package crab boil	2	tablespoons fresh parsley, chopped
2	stalks celery, chopped		
2	medium onions, quartered	1½	cups half and half
		1½	teaspoons salt
	Salt and pepper to taste	¼	teaspoon pepper
½	cup unsalted butter		Hot sauce to taste
1	medium onion, chopped	1	package long grain and wild rice (6 ounces), cooked
¼	cup all-purpose flour		
6	ounces sliced mushrooms		
1	cup chicken stock		Slivered almonds

Boil duck with crab boil, celery, onions, salt and pepper in water to cover for 1 hour or until tender. Debone and coarsely chop duck meat; set aside. Preheat oven to 350 degrees. Sauté onions in butter, then stir in flour, mushrooms, stock and wine. Add duck, parsley, cream, salt, pepper, hot sauce, and cooked rice. Place in 2-quart casserole, sprinkle with almonds, and bake for 25 to 30 minutes.

DUCK GUMBO

Submitted by: Chad Brauer

½	cup vegetable oil	1	small tomato, chopped
1	green pepper, chopped	1	teaspoon salt
½	cup flour	4	slices bacon, chopped
1	clove garlic, minced	1	bay leaf
5	stalks celery, chopped	½	teaspoon thyme
1	pound okra, sliced	½	teaspoon rosemary
2	medium onions, chopped	½	teaspoon red pepper
1	tablespoon vegetable oil		flakes
1	quart chicken broth	2½	pounds cooked duck
1	quart water		breast, chopped
⅓	cup Worcestershire sauce		Hot cooked rice
2	teaspoons hot sauce		Gumbo filé (optional)
¼	cup catsup		

Combine ½ cup oil and flour in a large Dutch oven; cook over medium heat, stirring constantly, until roux is caramel-colored (about 15 to 20 minutes). Stir in celery, onion, green pepper, and garlic; cook another 45 minutes, stirring every 5 minutes.

Fry okra in 1 tablespoon hot oil until browned. Add to gumbo and stir well over low heat for 5 minutes. At this point, the mixture may be cooled, packaged and frozen or refrigerated for later preparation.

Add broth and next 11 ingredients; simmer 2½ hours, stirring occasionally. Add duck during last 10 minutes of simmering period. Remove bay leaf. Serve over rice. Add gumbo filé if desired.

Makes about 15 cups.

"A hunter's life, although dedicated in part to the killing of game, is inevitably involved in the world of nature. The hunter's pleasures, excitement, and, to a large degree, his success—all are influenced by his role as a naturalist, his awareness of his surroundings and of how the overall pattern of wildlife affects his days in the field."

—Charles F. Waterman

DUTCH OVEN GOOSE

Submitted by: Steve McCadams

1	young goose, with skin	3	tablespoons cooking oil
1	package long grain and	1	onion, quartered
	wild rice mix	1	bay leaf
1	teaspoon salt	1	teaspoon marjoram
¼	teaspoon pepper	⅓	cup beef bouillon

Prepare rice and stuff goose with it. Brown bird on all sides in oil in large Dutch oven. Add onion, bay leaf and bouillon to the pot. Sprinkle bird with salt, pepper and marjoram. Cover oven and place hot coals around and on top of it. Roast for at least 1¾ hours, until the thigh bone moves easily. Four pound goose will serve 4 to 6.

FRIED DUCK

Submitted by: Greg Brinkley

Sauce for fried duck

4	tablespoons of grape jelly	1	tablespoon of mustard

Cut duck in to ½-inch strips.

Roll duck in mustard.

Roll the duck in flour and deep fry.

GOOSE CASSEROLE

Submitted by: Brad Harris

Debone breast meat and slice thinly across the grain. Put on fajita seasoning and refrigerate overnight. Pan fry until brown. Smother with cream of chicken and cream of mushroom soups. Leave the seasoning on the meat. Bake at 300 degrees covered for 45 minutes.

PURE DELIGHT DUCK OR GOOSE
Submitted by: Charlie Farmer

Fillet breast meat from fowl. Merely skin breast area by making small incision with knife and then pulling away skin far enough off the breast so it can be cut cleanly from the bone with a small, sharp knife. We do not utilize legs or wings. Rest of bird can be discarded.

Tenderize fillets by pounding (outside on wooden picnic table is the best place to do this) with food mallet. The mallet also opens up small holes in the meat. These small punctures better accept our favorite marinade, lemon pepper with lemon juice. With adequate time, we marinate/refrigerate overnight in crockery bowl with the fillets covered with lemon pepper. However, if we are craving fresh mallard or teal steaks the same day we bagged them, we simply rub the marinade into both sides of the fillets and grill over a hickory charcoal fire. There is a slight taste difference in all-night marinade and the rub-in version, but not much. The taste is delicious either way. We use NO OTHER SEASONING in this recipe.

One of the reasons wild duck and goose is commonly tough and chewy is that it is often over-cooked. It is important to watch the fillets on the grill. When all briquettes are full and glowing, that's the time to fire the fillets. Grill on each side until meat is medium brown. This usually takes 20 minutes or less. Meat should be slightly pink in the middle.

After meat cools slightly, lay fillets on a cutting board and use a long, sharp knife to cut the meat into thin (roast beef-type) strips. Lay the strips on a serving dish that matches the excellence of the meat itself. Garnish the plate with parsley, cherry tomatoes and a small, ornate, optional, dipping bowl filled with a horseradish sauce. Quite frankly, you don't need the optional sauce because the marinade and great flavor of wild fowl does it all. But some guests like the extra touch. Those who partake of this meat and recipe swear it is not wild fowl but rather some expensive cut of the finest beef. It can be devoured with fork or fingers.

DUCK KABOBS

Submitted by: Greg Brinkley

Slice duck into ½-inch strips.

Take 1 package of Italian season dry mix and mix as directed.

3	tablespoons of soy sauce	¼	teaspoon of cloves
3	tablespoons of lemon juice	4	cloves of garlic

Place duck and any other ingredients you desire (pineapple, bell peppers, onions) on skewer. Place on medium heated grill and cook for about 20 minutes.

It's best to have the meat next to the pineapple.

GRILLED DUCK BREAST

Submitted by: Chad Brauer

10-12	duck breasts	1	(16 ounce) bottle Italian dressing
1	cup jalapeño peppers, sliced		Toothpicks
1	red onion, sliced		

Butterfly cut each duck breast, then marinate breasts in Italian dressing for 2 to 3 days. Place 5 to 6 jalapeño slices and 2 to 3 slices of red onion into duck breast. Fold breast and use a toothpick to hold it shut. Grill over low heat for 25 to 30 minutes or until duck is fully cooked.

CHRISTMAS GOOSE

Submitted by: Bill Cooper

1	wild goose	¼	teaspoon pepper
	Peeled apples	¼	teaspoon salt
1	onion	⅛	teaspoon thyme
	Celery tops	⅛	teaspoon parsley
3	tablespoons butter	½	pint of your favorite red
1	teaspoon paprika		wine

Clean goose. Cover with salt and pepper. Fill cavity with raw apples, onion and celery tops. Close cavity. Cover in foil after adding melted butter, paprika, salt, pepper, thyme, parsley and wine. Roast in 350 degree oven. Baste often. Brown until done. Remove stuffing.

Serves 4.

HONEY-GLAZED WILD DUCK

Submitted by: Greg Hood

4	wild ducks	3	tablespoons honey
¼	cup margarine, softened	2	teaspoons reduced-sodium soy sauce
	Salt and pepper to taste		

Cut ducks into halves. Wash and pat dry inside and out. Rub with margarine. Sprinkle with salt and pepper. Place skin side up on rack in roasting pan. Roast at 350 degrees for 1 to 1½ hours or until tender. Brush with mixture of honey and soy sauce. Roast for 15 minutes longer. Brush with remaining honey mixture. Serve with wild rice.

MALLARD STIR-FRY

Submitted by: Mike Roux

Fillet three mallard breasts off the bone. This gives you six fillets. Cut these fillets lengthwise into strips about ½-inch thick. Coat a wok or deep skillet with a non-stick cooking spray. Brown the duck strips over a medium heat with ¼ cup diced red onion. Be careful not to overcook the meat.

When the strips have been thoroughly browned, remove them from the pan. Now add the following ingredients to the hot pan: ½ cup snow peas, ½ cup sliced water chestnuts, ½ cup sliced green bell pepper, ½ cup oriental style green beans. Heat the mixture over a medium heat until the veggies are heated through and through. (A time saving tip here would be to use a bag of frozen stir-fry vegetables from the grocery store).

Now put the browned duck strips back in the pan with the veggies. Add ⅓ cup of K.C. Masterpiece Honey/Dijon BBQ Sauce and heat for about five minutes. Serve over a bed of wild rice and add an egg roll.

DUCK WITH ORANGE SAUCE

Submitted by: Greg Hood

3	wild ducks	¼	cup thawed frozen orange juice concentrate
1½	teaspoons garlic powder		
1½	teaspoons onion powder	¼	cup packed light brown sugar
1½	teaspoons pepper		
6	lemons	2	tablespoons grated orange rind
6	oranges		
¼	cup margarine		

Rinse ducks, pat dry. Sprinkle each with ¼ teaspoon garlic powder, onion powder and pepper. Place each breast side up on 3 layers of foil. Squeeze juice of ½ lemon and ½ orange over each. Place half of each remaining lemon and orange in duck cavity. Wrap in foil, sealing well. Grill for 1 hour. Combine margarine, orange juice concentrate, brown sugar and orange rind in saucepan. Cook until thickened, stirring constantly. Place ducks on serving plate lined with greens. Spoon sauce over top.

DUCK IN RED WINE WITH DRIED FRUIT

Submitted by: Steve McCadams

2	tablespoons butter or margarine	½	cup (3 ounces) dried apricots
1	duck, 4 to 5 pounds, quartered, skinned and trimmed of fat	¾	cup (6 fluid ounces) dry red wine
6	shallots, finely chopped	1	cup (8 fluid ounces) chicken stock
2	cloves garlic, finely chopped		Salt and freshly ground pepper
½	cup (3 ounces) pitted prunes		

In a 4-quart heavy-bottomed pot over medium-high heat, melt the butter or margarine. Add the duck pieces, shallots and garlic and sauté, stirring, until lightly golden, about 10 minutes.

Pour off the duck fat from the pot and place the pot over medium-high heat. Add the prunes, apricots, red wine and chicken stock and, using a large spoon, deglaze the pot by stirring to dislodge any browned bits from the pot bottom. Reduce the heat to medium-low, cover and simmer gently for 30 minutes.

Turn the duck pieces over, cover again and continue to simmer gently until the duck is tender and cooked through when pierced with a sharp knife, 30 minutes longer. Season to taste with salt and pepper. Spoon into warmed shallow bowls and serve.

ROAST MALLARD

Submitted by: Charlene Cooper

Place 1 mallard in cold water with 2 tablespoons salt for each quart of water. Let sit overnight, then dry thoroughly. Season cavity with salt, pepper, and celery salt. Fill cavity with chunks of apples, onions and celery. Toothpick strips of bacon to breast. Place duck in roaster, breast down. Cover breast with water. Cover and bake at 350 degrees for 3 hours, or until bird is tender. Remove ½ of liquid. Turn duck breast up and roast uncovered at 400 degrees until breast is browned. Serves 2.

ROASTED DUCK BREAST

Submitted by: Bill Cooper

	Breasts of 3 wild ducks	¼	pound butter
	Flour	1½	teaspoons poultry
	Salt and pepper		seasoning
½	cup celery, chopped	1	cup water
1	onion, chopped	1	package stuffing mix

Season flour with salt and pepper. Roll ducks, covering thoroughly. Brown in hot oil. Cook onions and celery in butter. Add poultry seasoning. Add 1 cup water. Stir in stuffing mix. Add water as needed. Place ingredients in small roaster. Put browned breasts over dressing. Cover and bake at 350 degrees for 1 hour. Serves 2.

EVEN I CAN COOK IT ROAST DUCK

Submitted by: Greg Hood

2	ducks (2½ to 3 pounds each), oven-ready	½	cup butter
	Salt		8 slices bacon
	Pepper		Juice of 1 orange
	Paprika	¼	cup water
			Orange slices for garnish

Wash ducks inside and out. With sharp knife, split ducks in half, cutting the breast and back lengthwise. Sprinkle well with salt, pepper and paprika. Melt butter in large cast iron skillet. When it is very hot, brown the ducks on the breast sides. Preheat broiler. Place duck pieces in a roasting pan, breast side up, and top each of the four halves with two slices of bacon. Place under the hot broiler until the bacon has browned. Remove from heat. Preheat oven to 350 degrees for approximately 1½ hours, basting with the pan drippings every 15 minutes. Remove from oven and let sit for a few minutes before carving.

REMINGTON ROAST DUCK

Submitted by: Steve McCadams

1	mallard duck, cleaned	½	teaspoon pepper
1	tablespoon dry, red wine	1	teaspoon celery salt
1	cup water	½	cup chopped celery
1	teaspoon salt	½	cup chopped onion

Place duck in roasting pan. Pour wine over duck and add water to pan. Sprinkle with salt, pepper, celery salt, chopped celery and chopped onion. Place in preheated 500 degree oven for about 20 minutes, until duck is brown. Cover pan, reduce heat to 350 degrees and roast approximately 2 hours. Serves 2.

Recipe can be prepared in Dutch oven with hot coals piled on lid as well as under oven.

DUCK IN SOUR CREAM

Submitted by: Jessica Larson

2-2½	pounds duck	1	cup sour cream
	Flour seasoned with salt	½	cup water
	and pepper to taste	¼	teaspoon thyme
¼	cup butter		
½	cup sliced mushrooms, sautéed		

Preheat oven to 325 degrees. Roll duck pieces in seasoned flour and brown quickly in butter in a large skillet. Transfer pieces to lightly greased casserole dish. Add sour cream and mushrooms to casserole. Add water to skillet, then pour into casserole. Sprinkle with thyme and cover tightly. Bake until meat is tender, about 1 hour. Serve with rice or boiled potatoes.

Serves 2 to 5.

Note: This recipe is particularly good for tough birds, as the sour cream acts as a tenderizer.

169

SMOTHERED WILD DUCK BREAST

Submitted by: Greg Hood

8	wild duck breast halves, skinned		Salt and pepper to taste
½	cup flour	1	(8 ounce) can mushroom pieces

Coat duck breast halves with flour. Brown on both sides in oil in skillet; drain. Sprinkle with salt and pepper; add undrained mushrooms. Simmer, covered, for 1 hour and 20 minutes. Serve with wild rice.

STUFFED TEAL

Submitted by: Charlene Cooper

1	teal (per person)	Strips of bacon
	Salt and pepper	Cooking oil
	Stuffing mix	

Clean teal. Rub each carcass with cooking oil. Salt and pepper. Prepare stuffing mix as directed on package. Fill cavities with stuffing. Wrap breasts of teal with strips of bacon. Roast in covered baking dish at 350 degrees for about 20 minutes. Do not overcook! Duck is most flavorful on the rare side.

> *"Outdoor activities generate more hot air than any other sport pursuit. If all the fish and game stories, all the tales of endurance and survival and the like were stuffed in an enormous plenum, with a big fan behind it, they easily would melt the polar ice cap."*
> —Joel Vance, "Confessions of an Outdoor Maladroit"

BUFFET WILD DUCK

Submitted by: Kevin Howard

5 **wild ducks, cleaned and dried**	**3** **red apples, cored and quartered**

Stuff ducks with apples. Place in large roasting pan.

1 **cup Burgundy**	**½** **cup water**

Pour liquids over ducks. Cover pan and bake in 325 degree oven for 2 hours or until tender. Pour off the juice and set pan of ducks in refrigerator until they are very cold (meat slices more easily). Place ducks on carving board and remove all meat from the bones. Slice meat into slivers and place in baking dish, cover and store in refrigerator.

Sauce (Prepare 2 to 3 hours before serving)

½ **pound butter, melted**	**⅓** **cup lemon juice**

Heat butter, stirring in half of the lemon juice, until hot but not boiling. Taste sauce which should be tart but not sour, add more lemon juice if needed.

¼ **cup parsley, chopped**	**½** **teaspoon prepared mustard**
¼ **cup green onions and tops, chopped**	**Salt and pepper**
1 **tablespoon Worcestershire sauce**	

Add seasonings to melted butter and stir well.

Put ¼ of the duck in serving casserole, season with salt and pepper, drizzle with sauce and continue until all are used. Cover and let stand unrefrigerated 30 to 60 minutes. Bake at 325 degrees for 1 hour. Serve with fried rice.

Fried Rice

3 **cups cooked white rice, chilled**	**¾** **cup green onion tops, chopped**
½ **pound pork sausage**	
Soy sauce	

Fry sausage in a heavy skillet until brown. Drain all but 3 tablespoons of grease. Add chilled rice and carefully mix into sausage. Cook over low heat until hot. Pour soy sauce over rice until each grain is brown. Turn rice into casserole, cover with foil and bake at 350 degrees for 30 minutes. Fold green onions into rice and serve.

WILD MALLARD RICE

Submitted by: Scott Bennett

4	mallard breasts, deboned and cut into 2 ounce pieces		Sage
			Oregano
		1	red pepper
	Garlic salt	1	yellow pepper
	Olive oil	1	medium sweet onion
2	cups wild rice		Parsley
	Salt and pepper	10	fresh mushrooms

Prepare wild rice seasoned to taste and take off heat. Slice red and yellow peppers, mushrooms and sweet onion. In separate pan, add just enough oil to coat the bottom. Season to taste and sauté on low heat until done, making sure contents are still firm.

Layer separate frying pan with thin film of olive oil. Put tablespoon of olive oil into pan and place over medium hot heat. Season oil with oregano, salt, pepper, sage and parsley. Move seasonings around until they start to cook (45 seconds). Place duck meat in pan and brown on both sides. Take duck meat and vegetables and place in wild rice; mix well. Place in 325 degree oven for 25 minutes.

"Most of the time sportsman's bag is his presence in the natural world, and he feels he is a part of it while his hunt lasts. His joy is largely in escape from his artificial environment and his absorption in a world of elemental needs, but complex relationships. As a hunter, he is a predator—a part of nature's balance, helpful in some instances but a predator who must regulate his own impact up on his surroundings."

—Charles F. Waterman

Biographies

TONY ALLBRIGHT
Pontiac, Missouri

Tony Allbright is president of Executive Guide Service on Bull Shoals Lake in Missouri. He is also the popular co-host of the St. Louis based KMOX Outdoor Show.

Allbright has served as the chairman of several major charity fishing tournaments in the St. Louis area. He was named as "Grandpa's Pro" for the large chain of Grandpa's Stores in the metro area. Tony has also worked as a sales representative for major tackle manufacturing companies.

Tony has operated Executive Guide Service for major corporations as well as individuals for over 15 years. He has entertained such clients as Pepsi Cola, Anheuser Busch and Bristol Myers companies.

Allbright can be reached at Pontiac Lodge, HCR 1, Box 4, Pontiac, MO 65729, or by phone at 417-679-4169. For reservations, call 800-633-7920.

SCOTT BENNETT
West Point, Mississippi

Scott Bennett grew up in the Ozark woods and streams of Missouri hunting and fishing with his father, Bud Bennett.

Scott is an accomplished turkey and white-tail hunting guide, hunting videographer and outdoor photographer. He served on the Missouri Board of Directors of the National Wild Turkey Federation for six years.

Scott has had four wild turkey grand slams along with numerous turkeys in the National Wild Turkey Federation's record books.

Scott was coordinator of the Annual Bud Bennett Memorial Missouri JAKES Hunter Apprentice School. He is a major supporter of youth outdoor programs.

Some of Scott's favorite hunts are whitetails during the rut and gobblers when they're hot. He enjoys hunting with a bow more than any other weapon. Scott also enjoys fly fishing for trout and bluegill, fishing for crappie during spawn and largemouth bass at night.

Scott is the National Sales Manager for Mossy Oak Camouflage in West Point, Mississippi.

JARED BILLINGS
Crystal City, Missouri

Jared Billings, 45, grew up in Crystal City, Missouri, a small town in Jefferson County along the Mississippi River. He spent many youthful days fishing the Plattin Creek, chasing squirrels on nearby Buck Knob Mountain and roaming the Mississippi and her sloughs.

He was heavily influenced by his late grandfather and great-aunt, Jack Toulouse and Lucille Hampel. His Aunt Lucille had a cabin for many years on the Castor River south of Marquand, one of Jared's favorite places to spend a summer weekend.

After serving in the Navy, including duty in the Tonkin Gulf during the Vietnam War, Jared returned home and attended nursing school, earning a degree as an RN, but he never lost his love of the outdoors.

His favorite outdoor pursuits include camping and smallmouth fishing on Ozark streams with his 20 foot "river-jon" and hunting spring gobblers in the Ozark hills. He also enjoys deer hunting and just about any other type of fishing.

He has written a regular feature for the "Outdoor Guide Magazine" called the "Outdoor Almanac" and has appeared as a co-host on the "Outdoor Guide Radio Show" on KTRS in St. Louis.

Billings is a life member of the NRA and a volunteer Hunter Education Instructor for the Missouri Department of Conservation, a member of the Missouri Outdoor Communicators, the NWTF, the Missouri Smallmouth Alliance and many other outdoor organizations. He was the organizer and chairman of the 1997 U.S. Open Wild Turkey Calling Championship in St. Louis.

DAVID BLANTON
Columbus, Georgia

Georgia's David Blanton is no stranger to the outdoors. Blanton holds the enviable position of videographer for Realtree Outdoors.

David often slips from behind the camera to pursue game with gun and bow. David is a smooth-talking southern gentleman who often appears on video with Bill Jordan. David is also a regular on TNN Outdoors.

The popular Realtree hunting video series "Monster Bucks" is available at major outdoor equipment stores, or by calling 1-800-992-9968.

CHAD BRAUER
Camdenton, Missouri

Chad graduated from the University of Missouri in 1995 and holds a Bachelor's Degree in Fisheries and Wildlife. His area of specialization is in Bass Ecology. He is an experienced fishing guide on the Lake of the Ozarks in Missouri, and is currently in his third season on the B.A.S.S. and FLW tournament trails. Chad is the second generation of Brauers to enter the bass fishing arena; his father, Denny Brauer, is regarded as one of the best bass fishermen in the world. Chad registered his first victory as a bass fishing pro in October, 1996 by winning the BASS Tennessee Top 100 on Old Hickory Lake. To his win, he has also added four other top 10 finishes. Chad is currently sponsored by Ranger Boats, Evinrude Motors, Strike King Lures, Stren Fishing Lines, Plano Tackle Boxes, and Humminbird Electronics.

DENNY BRAUER
Camdenton, Missouri

Since starting full-time professional tournament bass fishing in 1980, Denny Brauer has established himself as one of the genuine superstars of the sport, and has become one of the most respected anglers in America.

An eight-time winner on the highly competitive B.A.S.S. tournament trail, Brauer earned the coveted B.A.S.S. Angler of the Year title in 1987. He also holds the record for the single season money winnings on the same circuit. He recently joined the Million Dollar Club on the B.A.S.S. circuit.

Denny is an active seminar speaker. He has been a guest on numerous television and radio programs and has starred numerous times on Bassmasters TV. He also has two videos on the market to help educate people on the sport of bass fishing and two books titled *Denny Brauer's Winning Tournament Tactics,* and *Denny Brauer's Jig Fishing Secrets.* He also designs lures and tests new products. Denny also won Bass Pro's Second Annual Legends Tournament in 1999.

Denny Brauer is currently sponsored on the professional bass fishing circuit by: Ranger Boats, Evinrude Motors, Daiwa Rod and Reels, Strike King Lures, Stren Fishing Lines, Chevy Trucks, Plano Tackleboxes, Humminbird, Dual Pro Charger, and Mustad Hooks.

In 1998 Denny Brauer distinguished himself by becoming the leading money winner on the B.A.S.S. circuit and by being the first fisherman to appear on the "Wheaties" cereal box.

GREG BRINKLEY
Marion, Arkansas

Greg Brinkley is a 6th grade teacher in the West Memphis, Arkansas School District. He likes to hunt ducks and deer. Brinkley currently hunts the Arkansas and Tennessee areas. He began building calls "to make a call that would hit the highest to the lowest sound and still sound ducky." Brinkley said he now understands why it is hard to tell someone how to make calls because of the hard work it takes. Brinkley enjoys swapping calls and is currently a member of the Call Makers and Collectors Association.

Greg knew what he was looking for when he began building calls in 1995. His first inspiration was in the first call he made. He and his dad worked on it all night and finally it made a buzz sound. The challenge was set and he began the task to make his own calls. Now, Greg turns approximately 150-200 calls annually from osage orange, cocobola, acrylics and many other domestic and exotic woods. He currently makes an Arkansas style call to achieve the highball and low end that ducks cannot resist. Brinkley taught himself to blow a duck call at the age of 14. He started duck hunting at the age of 7 and still loves it today. He is currently preparing for competitions and is seeking those interested in blowing his calls in competition. His calls are 100% guaranteed. To order duck calls from Greg Brinkley write to him at: 167 Military Road, Marion, Arkansas 72364; or call 870-739-1602; e-mail dukhntr@aol.com.

TAD BROWN
Columbia, Missouri

As production manager for M.A.D. Calls and a member of the Drury/Impact team, Tad Brown's contributions are immeasurable. His innovative ideas in call designs have helped to make M.A.D. Calls one of the premier call companies in the market today. A longtime resident of Warsaw, Missouri, Tad and his wife Pat have just recently moved to Columbia, Missouri. Tad's hobbies include hunting, trapping, and traditional muzzleloading. Tad enjoys hunting varmints, turkey, whitetail deer, and waterfowl.

JIM CASADA
Rock Hill, South Carolina

Jim Casada is a son of North Carolina's Great Smoky Mountains who enjoyed a marvelously misspent childhood thanks to growing up in a fly fishing family. He has enjoyed the pleasures of having a fly rod in hand for 50 of his 56 years. Along the way, he earned his B.A. in history at King College (Bristol, TN) in 1960, an M.A. in British history at Virginia Tech (1968), and a Ph.D. in British imperial history at Vanderbilt University (1972). He was Professor of History at Winthrop University in Rock Hill, SC for 25 years before taking early retirement to become a full-time writer. As a scholar he produced several books and upwards of 100 scholarly articles on African exploration.

He has been writing on the outdoors for almost two decades. Currently, Casada serves on the staffs of a number of regional and national magazines. He has written upwards of 2,000 feature articles for magazines.

Casada is the author or editor of some 15 books, including the award-winning *Modern Fly Fishing*. He has won upwards of 80 regional and national awards for his writing and photography. He annually teaches fly fishing classes in the University of Tennessee's non-credit program, the Smoky Mountain Field School, with Classic Sports International in Montana, and in "The Great Montana Fly Fishing Getaway."

Long active in writer's organizations, Casada is a past president and board chair of the Southeastern Outdoor Press Association, and he currently serves as President of the Outdoor Writers Association of America.

DAWN CHARGING
Garrison, North Dakota

Dawn Charging, is a full time freelance outdoor writer/photographer and upland guide who hails from the fields and prairies of North Dakota. Her work has been published in hundreds of regional and national magazines including "Bass Pro Shops Outdoor World," "Field & Stream," "Outdoor Life" and "In-Fisherman" magazines. She has been hunting waterfowl since she was knee-high to a magnum goose decoy, as her mother would take her hunting and hide her and her brothers and sisters under magnum goose decoys...it was an early beginning to a lifetime of hunting adventure in the great outdoors.

As an accomplished hunter, she has made guest appearances on numerous national hunting shows, North American Outdoors, ESPN, Babe Winkelman's Outdoor Secrets, and Tony Dean Outdoors. Dawn has also served as a pro staff member for outdoor products companies.

She is married to professional walleye angler, Johnnie Candle. Together they have become known as "The Outdoor Couple." They have recently moved to a log cabin (almost in the woods) along the shores of Lake Sakakawea and her family's resort, Indian Hills Resort, in Garrison, North Dakota.

Dawn is a member of the Outdoor Writers Association of America, the Association of Great Lakes Outdoor Writers, and the Native American Journalists Association. She also serves on the State Committee for Becoming an Outdoors Woman.

BILL COOPER
St. James, Missouri

Bill Cooper simultaneously earned a Master's Degree in Outdoor Recreation and an Officer's Commission in the US Army at the University of Missouri-Columbia. He graduated as a Distinguished Military Graduate. Bill has worked as a park superintendent, park naturalist and Director of Interpretive Services. He has been a free-lance outdoor writer for 25 years. His articles have appeared in "Game & Fish Publications," "Turkey Call," "Turkey and Turkey Hunting," "Rifle and Shotgun," "Outdoor Guide," "River Hills Traveler," and others.

"Outdoors with Bill Cooper" radio programs have aired across southern Missouri for three years. Top outdoor celebrities are often guests on his shows.

Bill is a certified professional by the Missouri Park and Recreation Association. He, along with his wife Charlene, serves on the George C. Clark State Board of the National Wild Turkey Federation. Both are certified Hunter Education Instructors and serve as the directors of the Bud Bennett Hunter Apprentice School. Both Bill and Charlene are members of the Hawkins Scent and Call Company's Pro Hunting Staff.

Bill is a member of the Outdoor Writers Association of America and was the president of the Missouri Outdoor Communicators for 1998-99.

He has taught Hunter Education courses and outdoor education classes in parks and resorts. He has also taught at the NWTF's "Women in the Outdoors" classes as well as the "Wonders of the Outdoor World" school sponsored by Bass Pro Shops, MDC, MDNR, USFS, University of Missouri Extension Service.

Bill is the editor of the *Outdoor Celebrities Cookbook*. And, just as he closes each radio program, he offers the following advice: "The next time you are enjoying your favorite outdoor activity, pause for a moment and give thanks to the Creator for our great outdoors!"

CHARLENE COOPER
St. James, Missouri

Charlene Cooper is a native Ozarkian originally from Steelville, Missouri, right in the heart of clear-water stream country. Charlene was raised on a hill farm on the banks of Dry Creek, a tributary to the Huzzah, one of the finest small-mouth streams in the country.

Although Charlene's love of the outdoors comes naturally, she has made a name for herself in outdoor circles. Her fondest memories are those of her dad, Gene Halbert, carrying her across the creek on his back while coon hunting.

Charlene is an avid outdoors lady. An experienced turkey hunter, she sits on the George C. Clark State Board of the National Wild Turkey Federation. She serves as the State JAKES Coordinator and has organized numerous outdoor events for kids across Missouri. Charlene, along with her husband Bill, is a director of the Bud Bennett Hunter Apprentice School.

Charlene is a certified Hunter Education Instructor and is on the Pro Hunting Staff of Hawkins Scent and Call Company. Charlene has taught outdoor skills at many JAKES events.

COREY COTTRELL
Steelville, Missouri

Corey Cottrell has enjoyed the woods and waters of Crawford County, Missouri since being born there in the summer of '69. The main attractions for Corey are the three rivers - the Huzzah, Courtois, and Meramec. These streams are not only at the heart of his family's business, but it was these waters that sparked Corey's interest in fishing, hunting, and the great outdoors.

Corey's only absence from Steelville was to obtain his Bachelor's degree in Parks, Recreation, and Tourism from the University of Missouri - Columbia in 1992. After graduation, he immediately returned to his hometown. His education has been very useful in his position at Huzzah Valley Resort, a booming business started by his family nearly twenty years ago. Corey balances his time between the rivers, the woods, the resort, and his wife. Corey is a true outdoorsman in every sense of the word. He considers himself one of the luckiest people alive to be minutes away from the things in life he truly enjoys.

Corey Cottrell is one of the top smallmouth guides in the nation. He offers guided trips on the Huzzah, Courtois, and Meramec Rivers in the beautiful Missouri Ozarks. To arrange a fishing trip with Corey, or a camping trip, float trip or trail ride call Huzzah Valley Resort at 573-786-8412.

BILL DANCE
Collierville, Tennessee

Bill Dance has won 23 National BASS titles and qualified for the Classic 8 out of 9 years. He was named Angler of the Year in 1969, 1974, and 1978. He also earned the Congressional National Water Safety Award in 1978. Bill was added to the National Freshwater Hall of Fame in 1986.

Bill has written seven books on fishing. His articles have been published in most major outdoor magazines including "Sports Afield," "Field and Stream," and "BASSMASTERS."

"Bill Dance Outdoors" has aired since 1986 with over 2,000 shows in its history. Bill has produced over 20 educational videos, and raised funds for numerous charities.

Bill Dance is sponsored by a myriad of corporations including Chevrolet Trucks, Eagle Claw, Mercury Marine, Motorguide, Pradco Lures, Remington Arms, Wal-Mart and Zebco.

WOO DAVES
Spring Grove, Virginia

Woo Daves, of Spring Grove, Virginia is a 14-time BassMasters Classic qualifier and has placed in the top five finishers five times. Woo has won many other tournaments across the country. Woo is the only 3-time winner of the Master Fisherman/Promotion Award from the Frank Carter Company.

Woo is heavily involved with Pro-Am Team's Piers for Handicapped Fishermen Program, Hopewell, Virginia's Optimist Club-Kids Fishing Tournament, and Super Kids (group of adults who are mentally handicapped) in Southside, Virginia. Woo raised enough money to buy a 25-seater bus for their transportation needs. "That is my greatest accomplishment ever!" says Woo.

Woo's sponsors include: Tracker Marine, Zebco-Quantum, Stren, Motorguide, Zoom Bait, Humminbird, Plano, Bill Norman Lures, and Eagle Claw. Woo has three videos in the Bass Pro Series.

Woo also has a fan club: Woo Daves Fan Club, 19320 Brandon Road, Spring Grove, Virginia 23881-9013.

JIM DOUGHERTY
Tulsa, Oklahoma

Jim Dougherty of Tulsa, Oklahoma is one of archery's foremost bowhunting personalities and authorities.

An active bowhunter since 1951, Dougherty has taken over 350 North American big game animals representing 17 species, and 16 species of African big-game including the dangerous Cape buffalo. Recognized as an all-around outdoorsman, he has won 17 state, national and world wildlife calling championships for varmint, duck, goose, turkey and elk; has set seven I.G.F.A. fly fishing world records, and is an ardent shotgunner, waterfowler and spring turkey hunter.

A popular bowhunting writer, Dougherty is Hunting Editor of "Bow & Arrow Hunting" magazine, columnist for "Peterson's Bowhunting (Trails End)," Editor at Large of "Western Bowhunter," and has authored two books - *Varmint Hunter's Digest* and *Jim Dougherty's Guide to Bowhunting Deer*. More recently he has been selected as the Archery Editor for "Texas Game & Fish" magazine.

As past president of the prestigious Pope & Young Club and the American Archery Council, Dougherty has given freely of his time and efforts in support of archery and bowhunting. Frequently recognized by his peers for his accomplishments, his awards include: Professional Archer of the Year, National Bowhunter's Hall of Fame, California Archery Hall of Fame, and election to the S.C.I. Bowhunters Hall of Honor. In January, 1997 he was inducted into the Archery Hall of Fame.

Dougherty is a Consulting advisor and spokesperson to many leading outdoor firms including: API Outdoors, Easton, Hoyt USA, New Archery Products, Cabela's, Mossy Oak and Lohman Manufacturing. Dougherty participates in educational seminars nationwide. He is also involved in product design and testing.

MARK DRURY
Columbia, Missouri

Drury Outdoors, Inc. and M.A.D. Calls, Inc. are headed by Mark Allen Drury. As president and co-owner of these two companies as well as vice president and co-owner of Impact Productions, Inc., Mark has dedicated the last ten years of his life to bringing the outdoorsman the highest quality products available today. His experience with Advanced Marketing over the past eight years has given him insight into the hunting market that others in this field cannot claim. Mark resides in Columbia, Missouri with his wife Tracy and their two-year-old daughter, Taylor. Mark gets out on the golf course to relieve a little stress when time allows; his competitive edge, though, comes into play on the professional turkey calling circuit where Mark is a six-time world champion. Marks' greatest joy is hunting the wild turkey, elusive whitetail, and formidable wild elk.

To order M.A.D. Calls or videos call: 1-888-TEAM-MAD.

RALPH DUREN
Jefferson City, Missouri

Ralph Duren is a native of Jefferson County, Missouri. He joined the Missouri Department of Conservation in 1979 as a Wildlife Damage Control Agent. Ralph later became an Outdoor Skills Specialist and then a Hunter Skills Specialist.

Ralph co-authored the MDC Turkey Hunter Education Manual and the Trapper Educational Manual. He also co-wrote the MDC movie "It's Your Choice," filmed by Glenn D. Chambers for use in Hunter Education classes. Ralph has penned many articles for the "Missouri Conservationist," "Show-Me Gobbler" and numerous newspapers. Ralph now serves as a Public Relations Specialist for the MDC.

Ralph appears regularly on KOMU-TV's "Popper and Friends." He has also appeared on the Missouri Outdoors TV program, CBS Tom Snyder Late Show, CBS This Morning, The Nashville Network, Cable News Network, FX Cable Network "Breakfast Time Show," "Home Life Show" on ALTS Net and Family Net, and "The Tonight Show" with Jay Leno on NBC.

Ralph imitates the sounds of almost 70 birds and animals. He is a champion turkey caller and owl hooter. He was the 1997 World Quail Calling Champion. Ralph can be viewed on the Lake Ozark Home page under What's New - funlake.com.

TOM EVANS
Rockmart, Georgia

Tom Evans has been a freelance stock photographer and licensed captain/fishing guide for twenty years, working with what God made and what Mother Nature allowed him to use in weather and sunlight. He has been married to his wife, Beverly, for twenty-five years.

"I travel all over North America chasing tippets and tailfeathers," Tom said. "Within the back roads of America I look for wildlife, beautiful scenics, another great fishing spot and some very fine hunting. I truly am a blessed man. I always say, 'Half of the payment is being there.'"

Tom has more than fourteen hundred cover shots published. He works with most of the outdoor publications, ad agencies, and calendar companies.

RAY EYE
Hillsboro, Missouri

Ray Eye is one of our country's most renown living outdoor legends, and America's premier educator, entertainer, celebrity and expert in the world of hunting.

Among Ray's many accomplishments are co-authoring the benchmark turkey hunting book "Hunting Wild Turkeys with Ray Eye", and production of the award-winning video series, "Eye on the Wild Turkey." As a new addition to his video series of products, Ray has just released "Eye on the Wild Turkey - Sounds of Spring" audio CD. "Outdoor Life Magazine" says, 'Sounds of Spring' is the best recording we've ever heard of turkeys in the wild."

Through video, audio, radio and television and thousands of seminars, including the NRA's Great American Hunters Tour, Ray has helped educate millions of hunters on the tactics, ethics, and safety of hunting.

In addition, NRA, Winchester Ammunition, Yamaha, Liberty Rugged Outdoor Wear, Aimpoint Sights, Hunters Specialties, Walkers Game Ear, Moultrie Feeders, Flambeau Products Company, Remington Firearms, Gerber Knives and Rocky Boots have tapped into Ray's notoriety and knowledge to help promote their products.

Most important to Ray is the time he donates to the preservation and restoration of wildlife. Through the education of America's youth and by working closely with conservation organizations, Ray has, and will always, strive to preserve our priceless wildlife resources and the privilege of hunting and enjoying the great outdoors.

CHARLIE FARMER
Ozark, Missouri

Charlie Farmer has been a full-time professional writer, specializing in first-hand outdoor adventure magazine articles and books since 1969. He has lived in Ozark, Missouri for 20 years and in 1988 was named "The Conservation Communicator of the Year" by the Conservation Federation of Missouri for his outstanding contribution to the wise use of our nation's natural resources. He has written 11 books about fishing, hunting, camping, canoeing, backpacking, outdoor cooking and history.

Farmer's outdoor and conservation columns appear weekly in the Springfield, Missouri News-Leader and the St. Louis Tribune. He also co-hosts a popular weekly outdoor radio program originating from Springfield, Missouri called the "Outside Story". And he has served on the board of directors of the Outdoor Writers Association of America (OWAA). A versatile outdoors communicator with over a thousand magazine credits, he is also a video and television script writer specializing in outdoor adventure and conservation topics. A popular speaker, his passionate presentations highlight the history, unique beauty and importance of the Ozarks' natural resources and the varied wealth of healthy outdoor recreation adventures available in the region.

J. WAYNE FEARS
Heflin, Alabama

Wayne grew up in Alabama learning outdoor skills from his dad, who was a trapper. He is a wildlife biologist with degrees from Auburn University and the University of Georgia. For eight years he was the Forest Recreation Manager for a major paper corporation in Alabama where he developed one of the largest hunting operations in North America. It consisted of 220 hunting leases on a half-million acres of land; a hunting lodge offering guided whitetail deer and turkey hunts; guided hunts in Alaska, British Columbia, and Colorado; and outdoor skills schools. He then developed his own hunting business with three hunting lodges in Alabama. Since he began freelance writing in 1968, Wayne has had over 3,000 magazine articles published in leading outdoor magazines. He has also written 14 books on outdoor subjects. One of Wayne's books, *Hunting Whitetail Successfully,* has sold over 250,000 copies. He has received numerous professional awards, including the University of Georgia Distinguished Alumni Award, the Gun Writer of the Year Award, and many other awards for outdoor writing. He was also elected a member of the Explorer's Club for his work in the Arctic. Wayne is the editor of "Rural Sportsman" magazine.

KATE FIDUCCIA
Bellvale, New York

Kate Fiduccia is the Executive Producer of "Fiduccia Video & Film Productions." She is a graduate of Cornell University, with a degree in Business and Hotel Management.

Kate's love of the outdoors led her to leave the skyscraper megalopolis and join "Woods N' Waters." As a canoeist and hiker, Kate diversified her outdoor interests to include hunting and fishing. Soon after joining the "Woods N' Water" television series, Kate became the Executive Producer. Within six months, she was also co-hosting the program. Kate's warm personality appeals to both women and men viewers across the nation.

Whether she's shooting big game, demonstrating how to use a deer call, cooking up a wild game dish, breaking a round of sporting clay targets or fighting a silver tarpon — Kate leaves viewers wanting to see more. Many readers and viewers have expressed their gratitude for Kate's participation on the series. They often write how the "entire family watches the show now."

Kate is an active member of the Outdoor Writers Association of America and the New York State Outdoor Writers Association. She is the Food Editor for "Whitetail Strategies" and has written for "Outdoor Life" and "Deer & Deer Hunting" magazines. Most recently, she appeared on the CBS Evening News on a segment about women and hunting.

Kate is a multi-talented business woman and wears many hats within the companies she manages. Although Kate is always busy keeping tight reign on all aspects of five corporations, she still manages to get afield to enjoy the woods and waters.

PETER J. FIDUCCIA
Warwick, New York

Peter Fiduccia, host of the "Woods N' Water" television series, is recognized throughout the outdoor fraternity for his knowledge and skills of outdoor sports.

Peter shares his knowledge and skills with fellow outdoor enthusiasts through his nationally syndicated television series, freelance magazine articles, newspaper columns, consumer video line, radio program and through his first book, *Whitetail Strategies — A No-Nonsense Approach to Successful Deer Hunting.*

Peter is an award-winning writer and producer with active membership in the Outdoor Writers Association of America, the Rod and Gun Editors Association of Metropolitan New York, and the New York State Outdoor Writers Association. He is a Contributing Editor for "Sports Afield" and is also the creator and Consulting Editor of the nationally distributed magazine, "Whitetail Strategies." His deer hunting features and "Deer Doctor" columns regularly appear in each issue.

For twelve years, Peter's warm smile and approachable personality has encouraged thousands of outdoor lovers to request his autograph and to attend his clinics over and over again. Peter's seminars are extremely popular because they are interesting, informative and entertaining. He is readily accepted by sportsmen and women throughout North America as one of the nation's top whitetail deer experts.

BILL FLETCHER
Mountain Home, Arkansas

Bill Fletcher has been guiding on Norfork Lake in Arkansas for 33 years. Bill is ticketed as one of the greatest striper guides in the United States today. Bill is also tops when it comes to wipers, largemouth bass, and crappie.

In the off season, Bill works as a waterfowl guide in the duck-rich rice fields of eastern Arkansas.

To book Bill Fletcher call 870-425-5170, or write: Bill Fletcher's Guide Service, Rt. 8 Box 437, Mountain Home, Arkansas 72653.

BOB FOULKROD
Troy, Pennsylvania

Nationally known bowhunter, writer, guide, and having appeared in many videos and TV shows, Bob Foulkrod of Troy, Pennsylvania has hunted game all over the world. He has hunted from the frigid Arctic Circle to sweltering Africa. Foulkrod is considered one of the most adaptable bowhunters today. He has gained his vast knowledge the hard way, in the field and forest, through his past caribou and bear camps and the Pennsylvania Bowhunting School held at his lodge.

Foulkrod's success with many different species of game has gained him international recognition as a bowhunter and a consultant for leading manufacturers, such as Golden Eagle, Satellite, Bass Pro Shops, Bushnell Sports Optics, Game Tracker, AFC's, Hunter Specialties, Realtree, Streamlight, and many others.

For information about Foulkrod's school write: Bob Foulkrod, Golden Eagle Bowhunting School, RD1, Box 140, Troy, PA 16947; or call 717-297-4367; FAX 717-297-1056. Internet: http://www.webpagers.com/golden/foulk.htm

SHIRLEY GRENOBLE
Altoona, Pennsylvania

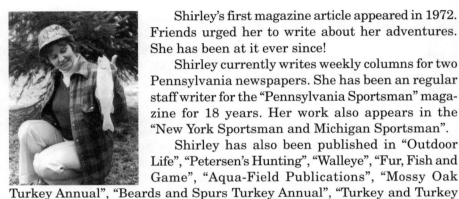

Shirley's first magazine article appeared in 1972. Friends urged her to write about her adventures. She has been at it ever since!

Shirley currently writes weekly columns for two Pennsylvania newspapers. She has been an regular staff writer for the "Pennsylvania Sportsman" magazine for 18 years. Her work also appears in the "New York Sportsman and Michigan Sportsman".

Shirley has also been published in "Outdoor Life", "Petersen's Hunting", "Walleye", "Fur, Fish and Game", "Aqua-Field Publications", "Mossy Oak Turkey Annual", "Beards and Spurs Turkey Annual", "Turkey and Turkey Hunting", and many more.

Shirley was the first female member of the Board of Directors of the National Wild Turkey Federation and the first (and so far, only) woman president of the NWTF's Pennsylvania chapter.

PAUL HANSEN
Gaithersburg, Maryland

Paul Hansen is Executive Director of the Izaak Walton League of America (IWLA), one of the nation's oldest and most respected conservation organizations. He started with the Izaak Walton League in January of 1982 as an Acid Rain Project Coordinator.

From 1981-90, Mr. Hansen also served as a consultant on acid rain and other bilateral environmental issues for the Canadian government's Department of the Environment and Department of External Affairs. In 1987, Canada's Speaker of the House of Commons, John Fraser, personally recognized Mr. Hansen on the floor of the Parliament as an "American Friend of Canada," for his work.

Mr. Hansen is the author of several IWLA reports and is active with a number of associations, including The Wildlife Society, the Outdoor Writers Association of America, and the International Association of Fish and Wildlife Agencies. He has testified before committees of the U.S. House of Representatives and Canada's Parliament, in addition to numerous state legislative and regulatory proceedings. He is currently on the board of the League of Conservation Voters, and is chair of the Expert Review Panel of the Sustainable Forestry Initiative.

BRAD HARRIS
Neosho, Missouri

Brad is a native Missourian and Vice-President of Public Relations for Lohman Game Calls. He has been an avid outdoorsman for over 30 years. He has taken many trophy animals with several Pope and Young qualifiers. An avid game caller, Brad has won numerous awards in turkey, owl, elk and predator competitions and is known as one of the top all-around game callers in the country. He has won several Grand Slam awards in turkey hunting, and has successfully hunted big game all over the United States, Canada, Mexico, and Africa.

Brad developed the first Grunt Deer call, the Turkey Tracer slate call and the Antelope Challenge call, which have set standards in the game calling industry. Brad also is a member of the Realtree pro-staff and Golden Eagle shooting staff.

Brad has produced the popular Real Hunting video series featuring turkey, deer, elk, predator, waterfowl and African Plains game. He also hosts "Lohman's Outdoor Traditions" television show. Additionally, he co-hosts the national radio program, "The Christian Sportsman."

Lohman products and videos can be ordered from Lohman Manufacturing Co., Inc., Box 220, Neosho, MO 64850; 417-451-4438; FAX 417-451-2576.

KYLE HICKS
Baton Rouge, Louisiana

Kyle Hicks of Baton Rouge, Louisiana, is on the Hunter's Specialties Promotional Staff. Since 1991 he has been a country singer, performing concerts with Hank Williams, Jr., Lynyrd Skynyrd, Merle Haggard and others. Kyle is an avid hunter and fisherman and a former rodeo participant.

Growing up in the rolling hills and swampy bottoms of Mississippi and Louisiana, he took his first buck at age 8. Kyle taught himself how to turkey hunt, calling in his first gobbler at age 13. He honed his skills, placing third in the Bayou Classic Open Competition and third runner-up in the Louisiana State Turkey Calling Contest.

Kyle has been active in supporting St. Jude's Children's Research Hospital and the Children's Miracle Network. He loves to introduce young people to hunting.

Hunter's Specialties is the largest manufacturer of hunting accessories. They produce a variety of products, including deer scents, turkey calls, camo items, and elk, waterfowl, and archery accessories.

GREG HOOD
Clarksdale, Mississippi

Greg Hood enjoys duck calling competitions, hunting, fishing and coaching baseball. He hunts in Canada, Missouri, Tennessee, Arkansas, Nebraska and his home state of Mississippi.

Hood loves working with wood. He uses cocobolo, black African wood, tulipwood, ebony, Mediterranean and olive woods to make his duck calls. He also uses acrylic and corian, the material that won Hood's world championship. His design is the Arkansas style.

In 1985, Hood won the national contest and other open contests in turkey calling. In 1987, he began duck calling in competition and in 1988 won the Mason-Dixon from Maryland, and placed fifth in the world and appeared on ESPN. He was also awarded a plaque from Governor Bill Clinton as an ambassador to Arkansas.

In 1989, Hood won the South Regional in Atlanta, and appeared on ESPN and "Tennessee Outdoorsman." In 1990 and 1991, he won the Tennessee State Championship Duck Calling Contest in Nashville and became one of the few people to ever hold the state title twice. In 1994, he began training callers in Mississippi, one being his sister, Lucy Lee McLain, who now holds the title "Women's World Champion" and the first woman ever to hold the title in Mississippi.

In 1995, the Mississippi legislature awarded Hood a commendation for his efforts in promoting and contributing to the wildlife resources, safety in hunting and for the future of generations to come.

To order one of Hood's calls, write: Greg Hood, 1275 Craig Road, Clarksdale, MS 38614; or phone 601-383-2235.

KEVIN HOWARD
Elsberry, Missouri

Kevin Howard, owner of Howard Communications, Inc., specializes in public relations and communications in the outdoor industry. A freelance writer with credits in many publications, he has also been a script writer for a number of outdoor videos.

Howard grew up on a farm in Northeast Missouri and has been an avid shooter, hunter, and fisherman most of his life. While attending college, he was a member of the University of Missouri trap and skeet team and competed all over the country.

After receiving a degree in animal nutrition, he worked in the agricultural business for several years as a manager of a grain and feed elevator.

In 1980, he began writing a weekly outdoor column for the "Louisiana Press Journal" in Louisiana, Missouri. Encouraged by friends and family, he quit his job at the elevator in 1983 to start his own outdoor publication in St. Louis. He served as publisher and editor of "Outdoor News" from 1983 to 1991 when he sold the business to pursue a full-time career in public relations.

Howard has worked with many companies in the outdoor field including Winchester Ammunition, Bushnell, Birchwood Casey, Midway Arms, and Motorola. Howard's background enables him to look objectively at what makes a good working relationship between companies and writers.

You may reach Kevin by phoning 573-898-3422 or writing Howard Communications, Inc. 289 Highway CC, Elsberry, MO 63343; e-mail: howcom@inweb.net.

TIM HUFFMAN
Poplar Bluff, Missouri

Tim Huffman is a writer/photographer. His works include both regional and national hunting/fishing articles, but he is best known for his crappie fishing photos and stories. He takes pride in turning information learned from national tournament teams, guides, experts and other top sources into practical how-to information for the weekend and/or serious fisherman. He has recently published three books and his columns appear regularly in the magazines "Outdoor Guide," "Big River Outdoors," and "Crappie."

Tim's hobbies are many, but at the top of the list are deer hunting, any type of fishing and family activities. He and his wife, Marty, have two sons, Landon and Travis.

Tim's books are available by sending a check or money order along with the title of the book(s) to: Huffman Publishing, P.O. Box 26, Poplar Bluff, MO 63902. Copies can be autographed for personal use or for gifts available upon request.

If you wish to order one of Tim's books, the following list contains descriptions and prices:

Winning Crappie Secrets, Slow Vertical Trolling. Features the techniques, tips and tricks of 1995 and 1997 Crappie Classic Champs Ronnie Capps and Steve Coleman. The cost of the book plus shipping and handling is $10.50.

Wappapello Sportsman's Guide. The cost of the book plus shipping and handling is $8.00.

Seasonal Structure for Crappie (1998). Detailed, how-to fishing guide for matching structure to the season, baits, and best techniques for year-round catching. The cost of the book plus shipping and handling is $11.50.

CASEY IWAI
Laveen, Arizona

Casey Iwai is a poised and articulate seventeen-year-old from Laveen, Arizona who began fishing at age five. Instantly fascinated by the sport, Casey learned everything he could from books, magazines, television programs and seminars. At age eight, he wrote a monthly column for kids for the "Arizona Fishing News Magazine." At eleven, he began fishing local club tournaments; at fourteen, Casey and a team partner, Steve Metherell, won a major state tournament. Casey took big bass honors with an eight pounder. The team placed fourth overall for the season and were honored as Allstar Bass Rookie Team of the Year for 1997.

At age eleven, Casey began conducting seminars on Buck Potter's Bass Bin at the Annual Phoenix Boat Show. Casey appeared at the Bass Pro Spring Classic in Springfield, Missouri, when he was fourteen. While he was there, he appeared on a discussion panel with Tommy Martin, Stacey King, Woo Daves, Penny Berryman and other fishing notables. Currently, Casey has begun to fish in the WON BASS and Angler's Choice Pro/Am tournaments in the west. Despite his busy schedule, Casey has also found time to be elected a senator at his high school and make an instructional video called, "Fish Hard, Fish Smart." He is sponsored by Nitro Boats, Tracker Marine, Action Marine, Humminbird and Enders Rods.

BRIAN JENKINS
Poplar Bluff, Missouri

Brian was born and raised in southeast Missouri. At an early age Brian loved to tinker and develop his ideas. His talents blossomed when he began making outdoor products.

Fortunately, Brian teamed up with a lovely business-minded lady who became his wife. Together, Brian and Jamie own and operate Hawkins D.O.A. Company.

Hawkins set a new standard in the scent industry in 1989, when they introduced the first scents on the market that do not spoil or freeze. Original Buck Draw, Buck-N-Doe, Signature of Dominance, and Out-Fox-Em are scents utilized by many of the top hunters today.

Hawkins' line of deer and turkey calls are unique in the industry. Many are made of natural woods and wild cane.

Hawkins carries a variety of hunting accessories and a full line of clothing. For a look at some unique outdoor products by Hawkins call 573-686-2657 or 1-800-686-6614 for a free catalog.

BILL JORDAN
Columbus, Georgia

Outdoor life has always been important to this Columbus, Georgia native, whether playing football, hunting or fishing. Jordan graduated from Ole Miss with a degree in business administration and returned to Columbus to join his family's boat dealership.

As an avid outdoorsman, Jordan recognized the need for improvements in outdoor clothing and gear. This led first to his forming a company to produce a limited line of accessories, then to his development of the Realtree and later Advantage and Woodland Plus camouflage patterns.

Today, Realtree has its own video production company, Realtree Outdoor Productions. This division of Realtree produces the company's television series, titled "Bill Jordan's Realtree Outdoors," which airs across the United States on TNN. The show is hosted by Jordan and airs for 26 weeks each year.

In 1994, Jordan created Team Realtree, a signature line of clothing and accessories that has become the uniform of hunters nationwide. Also in 1994, Jordan started a second camouflage company, Advantage Camouflage, Inc. After Advantage's first year it was second only to Realtree in the camouflage market.

In 1997, Jordan introduced Woodland Plus camouflage, essentially the same woodland camouflage hunters have known for years PLUS limb and leaf overlays.

One of Jordan's hobbies turned business is auto racing. In 1996, Jordan teamed with Richard Childress Racing, sponsoring their #31 car for five races. Realtree now has their own race car.

To receive a Realtree catalog, phone 1-800-992-9968.

KEITH KAVAJECZ
Kaukauna, Wisconsin

Keith Kavajecz is a professional walleye angler. Having fished since he was 3 years old, (Grandpa used to take him white bass fishing on the Fox River), Keith has enjoyed angling and the outdoors basically all his life. One of the top-ranked anglers in the country, Keith speaks at many of the large sport shows around the country when he's not in pursuit of walleye.

One of the main influences in Keith's cooking came from his background as a cook at Chinese restaurants during high school and college.

ROB KECK
Edgefield, South Carolina

Since 1981, Rob Keck has been executive vice president/CEO of the National Wild Turkey Federation. Even before he became the leader of the Federation, he was a noted turkey hunter and turkey calling champion, having been inducted into the Pennsylvania Turkey Hunting Hall of Fame and having won the Pennsylvania State, U.S. Open, and World calling championships by the age of 28.

Under his leadership the Federation has become one of the fastest growing single species conservation organizations in the country; membership has grown from 25,000 members in 1981 to over 200,000 today.

As a hunter, Rob has harvested a wild turkey in every state but Alaska, which has no wild turkeys. He's also turkey hunted successfully for Ocellated, Gould's and Rio Grande wild turkeys in Mexico, and throughout the North Island of New Zealand.

As a wildlife illustrator, Rob has donated original art pieces to the Federation that have helped raise hundreds of thousands of dollars for the NWTF's wild turkey programs His art has been featured in his column, Talk'n Turkey, which has run in "Turkey Call" magazine since 1977, and has graced the receivers of numerous Federation guns and blades of various knives. In addition to Talk'n Turkey, Rob has authored or co-authored chapters or forwards in five books.

As a wildlife personality, Rob has appeared as a guest on numerous national talk shows on network television as well as many hunting and outdoor shows on TNN, ESPN and other cable programs.

STACEY KING
Reeds Spring, Missouri

Stacey King grew up in Springfield, Missouri. He was about three or four when he began to show an interest in hunting and fishing and loved them both from the very beginning. He spends every free moment in the fall and winter hunting quail. At present Stacey owns five bird dogs that he has trained from pups. Stacey and the dogs spend many hours afield together.

Stacey acquired tremendous experience as a fisherman when he began guiding on Table Rock Lake, twenty-five years ago. From there he started fishing the B.A.S.S. tournaments and, at present, has qualified for the Bassmasters Classic seven times. Fishing has enabled him to travel all over the United States, Mexico and Canada and fish some fabulous lakes, speak at seminars, do TV and radio programs, magazine articles and videos. It also gives him an opportunity to work with youth organizations, charities and benefits. Stacey is a member of the Tracker Pro Team.

RON KRUGER
Benton, Kentucky

Ron Kruger has been a fixture on the outdoor scene for well over two decades. He started as an outdoor columnist for newspapers in the St. Louis and Southern Illinois areas. His work also has appeared in various regional and national outdoor publications.

Later, Ron served as the editor of the highly-respected, but short-lived, "Fishing & Hunting Journal". He also was the editor of the "Outdoor Guide" and the "St. Louis Labor Tribune" and for the "Outdoor Guide Quarterly" during the first year of its publication.

His passion for the outdoors is boundless. He worked as a hunting and fishing guide in the Ozarks for three years, then as a fishing guide on Kentucky Lake for seven years, where he still resides, guides and writes. Ron also owns a U.S. Patent on a fly/lure called the Desperate Diver that he makes and markets.

To arrange a fishing trip with Ron Kruger, call 502-354-8027.

JESSICA LARSON
Columbia, Missouri

Jessica is a graduate student at the University of Missouri-Columbia working on a master's degree in journalism with an emphasis in environmental reporting. In 1996, she received a bachelor's degree from the University of Tennessee-Martin in wildlife biology with a minor in English.

Jessica was born in Illinois, but soon her father's job moved her family out West, where she spent the first half of her life. After moving to the East coast, Jessica graduated from high school, then on to the South, where she earned her undergraduate degree. Jessica has grown to love moving to different places, for the diversity of cultures and opportunities to learn new things are entirely unique to each place.

Her father's career as a wildlife biologist and her mother's as a professor of English and Spanish really seem to have been combined in Jessica. She loves to write and is fascinated with wildlife, so it seemed natural for her to pursue a career as a wildlife journalist. Jessica hopes to help educate the American public about wildlife, including its beauty as well as the potential problems that can arise when civilization meets wilderness.

Along with writing about wildlife, Jessica also enjoys writing poetry and short fiction. She has found her studies, as well as her hunting experiences, to be exceptional material for both creative and informative writing.

Editor's Note: Jessica Larson is a talented outdoor writer aspiring to work for a major publication. She is available for employment and may be contacted at: 2868 Anfield Road, Raleigh, NC 27606.

JIM LOW
Jefferson City, Missouri

Jim Low is an outdoor writer by trade and a cook by inclination. He has and will eat nearly anything. He says this makes his culinary bent as much a survival tactic as a hobby.

Jim is the Print News Services Coordinator for the Missouri Department of Conservation. He moonlights as a freelance writer for a variety of magazines, including "Popular Lures," "Arkansas Wildlife," "Missouri Game & Fish," "Reptile and Amphibian," "Wild Garden," and "Australian Birding".

Jim is a member of the Association for Conservation Information, the Outdoor Writers Association of America and the Missouri Outdoor Communicators. He has been honored with seven Outdoor Ethics Writing Awards from the Izaak Walton League of America and has won a number of other awards for his writing and photography. He says his second-proudest accomplishment was founding the Grand Gulf Chapter of the National Audubon Society, which continues to thrive and play an active role in resource management issues in south-central Missouri 15 years later.

Jim and his wife, Diane, live in the midst of 40 acres of oak-hickory forest and cedar glades just outside Jefferson City, Missouri. They stay busy with vegetable and flower gardening, prairie restoration, forest management, hunting and occasional projects such as building a rock wall or a fish pond. As active members of Missouri Forest Keepers, they have taken inventory of every tree over 1-inch in diameter on their property. They keep a pretty close eye on the resident deer, turkey, squirrels, rabbits, songbirds and morel mushrooms, too.

JERRY MARTIN
Springfield, Missouri

Jerry Martin's passion may be calling turkeys in his native Ozarks, but it doesn't stop there. Since his hunting experiences began at age 8, Jerry has taken nearly every North American big game species. But his greatest hunting experiences revolve around recruiting new sportsmen. Favoring a bow or muzzle loader, his conquests include elk, mule deer, antelope, moose, bear and more than a dozen Pope and Young class whitetail bucks.

Jerry has appeared on numerous outdoor TV programs and video productions. He works as a hunting equipment buyer for Bass Pro Shops and is a member of the RedHead Pro Hunting Team.

STEVE McCADAMS
Paris, Tennessee

Crappie fishing is a way of life for National Crappiethon Classic Champion Steve McCadams. Steve and his partner won the "World Series" of crappie fishing by taking the Crappiethon Classic victory on Chickamauga Lake near Chattanooga in 1996. The most coveted title in all of crappie fishing paid them $56,500 in cash and prizes and added another feather to the cap of America's most popular crappie angler.

His ability to prove his point that crappie will take a bait any month of the year, has placed him in numerous magazines, newspapers and television shows across the country. He is a Crappiethon Classic Champion and has been labeled: "America's Best Known Crappie Fisherman."

As an outdoor writer and authority on crappie fishing he has co-authored a publication for "In-Fisherman" titled *Crappie Wisdom*. The book is considered to be the bible among the ranks of crappie anglers as it offers great detail, descriptive diagrams and photos. McCadams also does weekly radio programs and newspaper outdoor columns.

He holds a Bachelor of Science Degree in Biology and is an active member of the Outdoor Writers Association of America and past president of both the Tennessee Outdoor Writer Association and Southeastern Outdoor Press Association.

For guide service or your personal autographed copy of *Crappie Wisdom,* send $14.95 to Steve McCadams, 655 Anderson Dr., Paris, TN 38242; or phone 901-642-0360.

BOB McNALLY
Jacksonville, Florida

Bob McNally is a full-time professional outdoor writer/photographer/broadcaster living near Jacksonville, Florida. He has been a full-time outdoor writer since graduating from the University of Wisconsin in 1972.

In addition to his professional newspaper outdoor writing, Bob has written over 4,000 feature magazine articles for every important outdoor publication in the United States. McNally averages well over 150 magazine feature stories each year, for publications such as "Outdoor Life," "Field & Stream," "Sports Afield," "BassMaster," "Fishing World," and "Salt Water Sportsman." He is the author of 12 outdoor books, including the best-selling *Complete Book of Fishing Knots and Rigs, Bass In Depth,* and the soon-to-be-released, *Fishing Inshore.* He also is on the writing staffs of "Southern Outdoors," "Outdoor World," "Florida Sportsman," and "Fishing Facts" magazines. For 3½ years Bob hosted the syndicated "In- Fisherman Saltwater Radio Show."

McNally's writing, broadcasting and photography work have won over 150 state, regional and national awards, and he has appeared in numerous television and radio outdoor shows, and has done many outdoor seminars.

KAREN MEHALL
Fairfax, Virginia

Karen Mehall is a true outdoor enthusiast. An avid hunter, she has hunted with her father and brother for nearly 10 years, enjoying small game, wild turkey and waterfowl, but especially whitetail deer.

As someone who feels fortunate to have the opportunity to work in the area closest to her heart, she serves as editor of the National Rifle Association's publication "The American Guardian" where she promotes education and training programs and special events such as the Youth Hunter Education Challenge, Great American Hunters Tour, women's activities and national shooting championships. After getting a large eight-pointer last fall — her biggest buck yet — she proudly hung it in her office where it joins her in greeting her visitors to NRA.

Karen serves as an NRA Certified Firearms Instructor and enjoys doing interviews on behalf of the NRA on what it means to be a hunter and on promoting hunting and women's issues.

For Karen, the outdoors is about camaraderie, adventure and enthusiasm and is her number one source of mental refreshment and physical challenge. She enjoys introducing newcomers to shooting and hunting because she takes pride in the outdoors and has great appreciation for outdoor quality time.

Karen graduated from the University of Maryland in 1987 with a bachelor's degree in journalism and public relations. In her spare time, she enjoys playing the accordion, horseback riding, camping, hiking, fishing and spending time with family and friends. To reach Karen at the NRA, call 1-800-672-3888, ext. 1355.

NICK MUCKERMAN
Chesterfield, Missouri

Young Nick Muckerman is an avid outdoorsman and an up-and-coming outdoor writer with an impressive list of accomplishments for a 15-year-old. Nick's passion for hunting and fishing is obvious to anyone who has read one of his 20 published articles. Nick's writing career started when he was 11 years old and he continues to be the youngest staff writer for "Outdoor Guide," a regional Midwest publication based in St. Louis. Nick is also the youngest member of the Missouri Outdoor Communicators, an association of outdoor writers and photographers.

As a writer, Nick is a young man with a mission. Nick is an effective evangelist, inspiring kids to try fishing, shooting, and hunting. Nick's passion for the outdoors is contagious for both young and old. His stories invoke fond memories in seasoned sportsmen and suggest the mutual benefits of introducing a youngster to the lifelong enjoyment of the outdoor sports.

At age six when neighborhood kids set up lemonade stands, Nick set up a stand to sell fishing flies that he constructed from feathers and household materials. Since then, Nick has taken over forty hours of fly-tying classes. He is now a member of Ozark Fly Fishers and a masterful fly tier.

The only thing that Nick enjoys more than fishing is hunting. Whether it's frog gigging on hot July nights, calling in wild turkeys, dove hunting or bowhunting for boar in Texas, Nick epitomizes the determined predator. Nick is wise beyond his years, however, in his appreciation that there's more to hunting than just the harvesting.

Nick enjoys the anticipation, the preparation, the camaraderie of the hunting camp, as well as the thrill of the chase. For Nick, preparation has led to considerable involvement in the shooting sports and in hunter education. In 1998, Nick earned the prestigious position of Grand Champion of the NRA International Youth Hunter Education Challenge (YHEC), a four-day, eight-category event held at the NRA's Whittington Center in New Mexico. Nick is also the YHEC 1998 Orienteering Champion and the 1997 Junior Rifle Champion.

Nick Muckerman is a model for our youth and an inspiration for all sportsmen. Nick is the future of our great sport.

GREG NIXON
Quincy, Illinois

Greg Nixon's photographs and articles have been published in many regional and national publications. Besides wildlife photography, Nixon spends a great deal of time photographing for celebrities. He has worked for Mike Roux of "Great River Outdoors," Buck McNeely "Outdoorsman International" and photographed events like Irlene Mandrell's Celebrity Shoot.

Nixon recently put down his still camera for a video camera and produced a television program called "Eagles Along the Mississippi." This documentary on the American Bald Eagle received great reviews and a new episode is in the works. He is also the chairman of the "Eagle Watch" in Quincy, Illinois. This is a educational program to enlighten the public about the Bald Eagle as well as other birds of prey.

When Greg is not filming or photographing, he is bowhunting. Nixon has hunted coast to coast and in Canada for many big game species. He lives for bear hunting with hounds, over bait, or spot and stalk. Just as long as he is bear hunting, the method doesn't matter.

His passion for bear hunting was instrumental in leading him to publish "Bearhunter" magazine. This magazine covers all types of bear hunting including black bear, grizzly bear, polar bear and Russian bear. "Bearhunter" has articles including where to hunt, how to hunt, adventure stories, forecasts, legislative and anti-hunting updates. For more information, write to "Bearhunter" magazine, 12 Curved Creek Road, Quincy, Illinois 62301; phone 217-223-4512; FAX 217-4223-8744.

TED NUGENT
Jackson, Michigan

Ted Nugent began hunting in 1953, and playing guitar in 1956. To date, he has released 29 recordings, and sold over 30 million albums. Renowned as one of the world's leading guitar showmen, he is equally well known as one of the nation's preeminent media personalities.

Acclaimed for his bold, insightful commentary on issues ranging from gun control to biodiversity, Nugent is host of "The Ted Nugent Show," on WWBR, Detroit, and a regular guest on top-rated programs like "Politically Incorrect," and a guest on the shows of Larry King, Tom Snyder, Ken Hamblin, and Rush Limbaugh.

A recipient of numerous commendations from state police, sheriff departments, FBI and police agencies nationwide, Nugent has been lauded for his Ted Nugent Kamp for Kids and work as a national spokesman for D.A.R.E. He continues to fight for personal freedoms as Editor/Publisher of his "Adventure Outdoors" magazine, on the lecture circuit, and as an award-winning writer.

Ted is one of the most powerful voices today for the hunting and shooting sports. He reaches millions every day through the media. His "Spirit of the Wild" PBS video series has raised over $3,000,000 for PBS affiliates nationwide. Ted is a life member of many conservation organizations and was appointed to the Board of the National Rifle Association in 1995.

To obtain information about Ted Nugent's Kamp for Kids, write to 4133 W. Michigan Avenue, Jackson, MI 49202.

RICK OLSON
Mina, South Dakota

Enthusiasm and hard work have paid off in a steady climb up the walleye tournament ladder for Rick Olson. The 40-year-old South Dakota native received his first visibility as a tournament angler by winning numerous events throughout the Missouri River Reservoir system. The years that followed led Rick to prominent status on both the Professional Walleye Trail (PWT) and the North American Walleye Anglers (NAWA) tournament circuits. Rick's determination to be a champion has led him from the Rookie of the Year title in his first year following the pro tour to the World Championship title in 1994. Rick is one of the steadiest and most well-respected anglers on the pro tour. He has qualified for every championship field since joining the tour full time, and has accumulated 38 national awards, and he holds the all-time record for a one day catch in NAWA or PWT event with 6 fish weighing 54.96 pounds.

Rick's current sponsors include: Tracker Marine, Mercury Marine, Normark-Rapala/Blue Fox, ACDelco Voyager Batteries & Chargers, Luck 'E' Strike, Apelco-Raytheon Electronics, Motorguide, VMC Hooks, Bass Pro Shops & Walleye Angler Catalog.

WALTER PARROTT
Fredericktown, Missouri

Walter Parrott has won more turkey calling championships than anyone in the world! He is a 5-time Grand National Champion, 4-time World Title Champion, and 5-time US Open Champion. Walter has won dozens of other state and regional turkey calling championships.

Walter is a member of the prestigious RedHead Pro Hunting Team, the Mossy Oak Pro Staff, has a personal line of turkey calls with Knight and Hale, and is co-host of "Ultimate Deer and Turkey Hunting" with Chuck Jones.

Watch for Walter on Mossy Oak's "Hunting the Country" on TNN, Sunday evenings at 9 p.m. CST.

LINDSEY PEARCE
Newton, Kansas

Lindsey Pearce is a 15-year-old freshman. She's an honors student, plays viola in the high school orchestra and has been involved in dance for 11 years.

So far, she's successfully hunted whitetails, wild hogs, turkeys, geese, doves, quail, pheasants, rabbits, and squirrels. An Osceola will complete her grand slam on turkeys.

She's been raised on wild game and sees no reason to change. She once said she'd never marry a man who wouldn't eat the venison she brought home. Elk and dove are her favorites. Turkey hunting is her favorite in terms of excitement, but she really enjoys the fast action of a good dove hunt.

She trained her own beagle, Freckles, and likes target shooting. Her favorite gun is a Beretta 20-gauge Silver Piegon over/under. She also has a Browning .30-06 for big game hunting, a muzzleloader and an heirloom .22.

Though her school and extra-curricular activities keep her busy, Lindsey plans on taking one fall big game and one special spring turkey hunt with her father, Michael Pearce, every year. For her high school graduation present, Lindsey has asked for a dall sheep hunt in Alaska. Chances are sky high she'll get it.

She also likes to fish with spinning or fly fishing equipment. Her most memorable fish was a 110-pound sailfish on 20-pound test line. The battle lasted 45 minutes, the fish jumped over 30 times and Lindsey helped release it. Two summers she caught a number of 20-inch plus rainbows and browns while fly fishing in Montana.

MICHAEL PEARCE
Newton, Kansas

As an outdoor writer Michael Pearce has enjoyed over 1,600 by-lines, in a variety of publications from "Sports Illustrated" to the "Newton Kansan." Though he's been routinely published in most sporting magazines, Pearce may be best known for his work in "Outdoor Life" magazine, and outside the traditional "hook & bullet" markets.

In 1985, frustrated with seeing continuing anti-hunting messages in the general media, Pearce set his sights high and initiated a working relationship with the "Wall Street Journal." Since then Pearce has written scores of articles for the highly-respected publication, all on the outdoors. The articles have carried strong pro-conservation, pro-hunting and pro-firearm angles.

Many times Pearce's work has highlighted the positive effects hunting has on local economies, and how conservation practices for game animals benefits non-game populations as well. Through various ways, every sporting article has helped dispel many of the general public's misconceptions about the American hunter.

His efforts to spread the word to non-hunters won Pearce honors three of the four years of the prestigious Winchester "Good News On Hunting!" writing contest, with first place finishes in both newspaper and magazine categories. Pearce is still striving to bring such pro-sporting articles to non-traditional publications, and was recently named Contributing Outdoor Editor for "The Robb Report."

Within the past few years, Pearce has focused a great deal of his professional efforts on drawing more women and children into the outdoors. A contributing editor at "Outdoor Life," in 1997 Pearce initiated and is now authoring a first of its kind monthly column, "The Next Generation," which teaches adults how to best introduce youngsters to hunting, shooting and fishing.

WILL PRIMOS
Jackson, Mississippi

Will Primos made his first duck call at the age of eight. Little did he know that he would eventually make his living designing and manufacturing hunting calls and accessories for hunters and outdoorsmen.

As a young hunter, Will Primos was never satisfied with the game calls he bought. He knew he could do better. So, in 1976, he started what is known today as Primos Hunting Calls and Accessories. Since then, Will's singular motivation has been to produce calls that would perform perfectly in the woods.

In 1987, Primos began producing "The Truth®" video series as an entertaining salute to hunting by capturing the grace and beauty of animals in the wild outdoors. Featured hunts include successful harvests as well as those hunts where the animals came out the winner — actual hunts, as they really happened.

While Will has certainly contributed to the industry as a call maker and video producer, perhaps his greatest contributions have been as a sportsman and conservationist. He is proud to be on the Advantage® Camouflage pro staff and a member of the PSE Hunting Advisory Staff. He has always been a devout supporter of organizations that benefit hunters and wildlife and has used his position within the industry to promote sportsmanship and wildlife management.

For more information concerning Primos Game Calls, write to Will at PO Box 12785, Jackson, MS 39236-2785, or phone 601-366-1288.

STEVE PUPPE
Red Wing, Minnesota

Steve Puppe became a pro staff member of Hunter's Specialties in 1991, but his background goes back much further. Steve grew up in the midst of the wildlife-rich hills and valleys along the Mississippi River near Red Wing, Minnesota. Steve harvested his first whitetail deer at the age of 12. During his high school years he spent his free time hunting and trapping.

Steve specializes in the use of scents and lures and successfully using scent elimination products to outwit big bucks.

"You can fool a buck's eyes and ears, but it's a lot tougher to fool his nose," he says.

Steve has been featured on ESPN with Tom Miranda, Babe Winkleman's "Outdoor Secrets" and on the Joe Bucher television show, as well as in H.S. videos.

His hunting expertise landed him a full-time job with Hunter's Specialties as their promotional coordinator. Steve travels across the United States, conducting seminars and sharing his knowledge with other hunters.

Steve says that becoming a successful hunter means "spending as much time scouting as possible and learning every inch of the land that you can." He credits his success in harvesting mature whitetail bucks to knowing their habits and habitat. Steve also enjoys taking kids and new hunters afield so they can share in the great experience of the outdoors.

You can contact Hunter's Specialties at 6000 Huntington Court N.E., Cedar Rapids, Iowa 52402-1268 or by visiting our web site at www.hunterspec.com.

HANK REIFEISS
St. Louis, Missouri

The name Hank Reifeiss is synonymous with Ozarks smallmouth bass fishing. Hank is a top-notch fly fisherman with over 40 years of experience.

Hank is a staff writer for "Outdoor Guide" magazine, which covers seven mid-western states. He is also Conservation Director of the Ozark Fly Fishers.

Hank is best known as an Ozark river fishing guide. Just to watch Hank work his magic with a fly rod on a splendid Ozark stream will be an experience you will long remember.

ALEX RUTLEDGE
Birch Tree, Missouri

When it comes to game calling, Alex Rutledge is a tough act to follow. With over 15 years of hunting experience, Alex has called in turkey, deer and predators, and has competed successfully in numerous turkey calling contests.

In 1986, Alex won the National Amateur Turkey Calling Contest, held in Yellville, Arkansas. During the same year he was also named the Missouri State Turkey Calling Champion. In 1988, Alex won the Grand National Gobbling Championship in Atlanta, Georgia. In 1991, he was the top caller at the South Central Missouri Ozark Turkey Calling Championship and also won the South West Open Calling Championship, held in Little Rock, Arkansas.

Alex attributes his hunting and game calling skills to being raised in a hunting and fishing atmosphere in the Ozarks of south central Missouri. His knowledge of predator calling benefitted Hunter's Specialties when he helped design and field test their predator calls. When pressed to name his favorite hunting partner, Alex admits it is his wife, Lynda.

Alex constantly hones his outdoor skills by guiding hunters on archery and spring turkey hunts. He explains that his goal is to teach hunters as much as possible in his three-day hunts. As an H.S. Pro Staffer, Alex helps hunters choose the right equipment and develop hunting strategies. He also hosts hunting seminars for Hunter's Specialties, the world's largest manufacturer of camouflage and hunting accessories.

You can contact Hunter's Specialties at 6000 Huntington Court N.E., Cedar Rapids, Iowa 52402-1268 or by visiting our web site at www.hunterspec.com.

EDDIE SALTER
Evergreen, Alabama

Eddie Salter is recognized as one of the foremost authorities on turkey and deer hunting. Eddie began turkey hunting at the age of 8 near his home in Evergreen, Alabama. Gaining from the teachings of his father and grandfather, he called in and harvested his first gobbler at the age of 10. As he grew older, Eddie's hunting interests broadened to include deer hunting.

Eddie began competitive turkey calling in 1981. He has amassed an impressive list of victories, including four Alabama state championships and two World Championships. Eddie was voted one of the top 10 sportsmen in 1986 and 1989.

In 1985 he created Eddie Salter Calls, Inc., where he produced a line of turkey and deer calls, scents and videos. Eddie sold the company in 1994. In 1997, he joined the Hunter's Specialties Pro Staff, where his knowledge of turkeys and turkey calls in invaluable. Eddie now travels the country, sharing his experience with other hunters and promoting H.S. products.

Eddie recommends becoming proficient on several different calls. Learning to read a turkey and communicate with it is important. "If you get a very callable turkey, don't be afraid to be aggressive," said Eddie.

Eddie also enjoys spending time with his wife Julie and daughter Mallory. Fishing is one sport the entire family enjoys together. They also enjoy watching Braves baseball.

You can contact Hunter's Specialties at 6000 Huntington Court N.E., Cedar Rapids, Iowa 52402-1268 or by visiting our web site at www.hunterspec.com.

CHAD SCHEARER
Great Falls, Montana

As a licensed professional outfitter and guide in the state of Montana, and owner and operator of Central Montana Outfitters, Chad Schearer is making a life out of his dreams. When Chad was old enough to carry his gear, his father introduced him to the world of hunting and fishing. From that point on, Chad was hooked. By his teenage years, Chad knew that this was more than a hobby for him — hunting and fishing were a part of his life. He enrolled in the Montana Hunter Safety Education Program and became a junior instructor. A few years later, Chad became a State Hunter Safety Instructor and began his career guiding friends on hunts and calling in a variety of game. At age 27, Chad is not only an accomplished guide, world champion caller and professional speaker, but also one of the youngest licensed outfitters in North America.

As an outfitter, Chad's main goal is to give the client the highest quality hunting and fishing experience. Proving himself to be one of the best in his profession, Chad's clients include Patrick McManus ("Outdoor Life" magazine), Tim McGraw (country music recording artist), and Jeff Cook (member of recording group Alabama), just to name a few.

Chad is also an award winning game caller holding the title of 1997 World Elk Calling Champion for the Rocky Mountain Elk Foundation — Pro Division. Participating in regional, national and international competitions, Chad has walked away with honors from around the country.

Guided hunts may be arranged with Chad Schearer by writing P.O. Box 6655, Great Falls, Montana 59406.

STEVE STOLTZ
St. Louis, Missouri

Steve Stoltz has become one of the nation's leading hunting authorities. He is on the pro staff of Outland Sports - Lohman/M.A.D. Game Calls, Mossy Oak Camouflage, and Browning Archery. His expertise is whitetail deer and wild turkey. Steve is one of the most successful pro-turkey callers in the history of the sport, winning or placing in over 200 turkey calling championships including the 1993 World Championship and 1998 Grand National Champion of Champions. He is also a nationally known videographer with Drury Outdoors. With a wall full of trophy whitetails and wild turkeys to his credit, it is no wonder the Drury Outdoors & Impact Productions library of hunting films are the largest and most successful 100% Wild, 100% Fair Chase series in the United States.

JIM STRELEC
Cadiz, Kentucky

Jim Strelec is a nationally acclaimed seminar speaker. Whether these mini schools take place at major sports shows, small sportsmans' clubs, Alberta's deer classic, or about any group situation in between, the crowds are always captured by Jim's knowledge and his delivery.

Of all Jim's considerable wisdom, when it comes to calling and hunting, one of his prime specialties is calling. He comes by his know-how quite naturally, since he is the special promotional coordinator for Knight & Hale Game Call division of PRADCO in Cadiz, Kentucky. Jim says that one cannot spend 30 years around the likes of Harold Knight and David Hale and not acquire the ability to call. Jim uses this knowledge in his presentations to not only teach, but to entertain as well.

At the sports shows, Jim takes time to help others in the use of the calls and with their questions on other hunting related issues that they may have. It is the willingness to assist the average man that has made him a repeat speaker at many of the popular outdoor shows. Jim keeps himself up-to-date on all the newest equipment and innovations in the world of hunting.

RONNIE "CUZ" STRICKLAND
West Point, Mississippi

For the past 8 years, Haas Outdoors, Inc.'s public relations has gained new peaks. The success of this is due to a certain individual and his staff of creative, hardworking people.

Ronnie Strickland, at age 44, is a native of Natchez, Mississippi. He has been in the hunting and outdoor industry for 19 years. Involved in sales on a retail level for about 8 years, Strickland then took his expertise and a very successful record and ventured into video production.

In 1986 Ronnie teamed up with Primos Game Calls as a videographer and co-producer. Becoming nationally known as "CUZ" Ronnie co-produced more than 10 hit videos, including "The Truth About Turkey Calling Vol. 1 thru 6", "The Truth About Calling and Bowhunting Whitetails Vol. 1, 2, & 3", and "Focus on the Hunt."

Strickland hit the road selling in 1988 for a well known marketing group, Advanced Marketing Specialist, covering the state of Mississippi. In 1990, selling success, long hours and total dedication landed Ronnie the position of Public Relations Director for Haas Outdoors' corporate office in West Point, Mississippi.

Ronnie's department now handles all public relations and media services, the newest venture being producer of Mossy Oak's very own television series "Hunting the Country" which airs on TNN and the production of three videos—Mossy Oak's "Mega Buck's One," "Whistling Wings," and "Facts & Feathers."

In 1996, Ronnie was promoted to Senior Vice President of Media Services and Public Relations. Strickland's objectives are to oversee all aspects of Public Relations, Entertainment, and Video Production.

Ronnie, his wife Pam, and their two daughters, Amy and Lauren, reside in West Point.

KEITH SUTTON
Alexander, Arkansas

In 1985, after working as a park naturalist, ranger and Boy Scout executive, Keith Sutton began a career with the Arkansas Game & Fish Commission where he is editor of "Arkansas Wildlife" magazine. He is also a prolific free-lance writer and photographer, well-known in his native South. He has authored more than 800 articles published in "Field & Stream," "In-Fisherman," "Southern Outdoors," "Rural Sportsman," "Petersen's Hunting," "Bassin," "Bass Fishing,"," "North American Hunter," "North American Fisherman," "Crappie World," "Game & Fish Publications," and many other state, regional and national periodicals. He has written all or part of 11 books (including four game & fish cookbooks), and his works as an award-winning photographer have been featured in a broad spectrum of books, magazines, newspapers and calendars.

Off-beat subjects are his specialty. While most outdoor communicators focus their attention on deer, bass and other popular species, Sutton teaches about lesser-known game and fish like swamp rabbits, flathead catfish, rails, alligator gar and snipe. His writings on outdoor ethics, nature, wildlife conservation and family recreation have been recognized by the Izaak Walton League of America and Outdoor Writers Association of America as among the best in the nation.

Sutton is a respected and recognized member of the outdoor writers' fraternity. He is vice president of the Southeastern Outdoor Press Association, served two terms as president of the Arkansas Outdoor Press Association, and is an active member of the Outdoor Writers Association of America.

STEVE "BOOMER" SUTTON
Cartersville, Georgia

In April 1997, "Georgia Outdoors" began airing nationally on the Outdoor Life Network. Additionally, "Georgia Outdoors" began airing in England, France, Germany, Italy and Spain in 1998. With such a large and growing audience, "Boomer" has the incredible challenge and responsibility of being a role model. Many of these viewers are children. "Boomer" believes that as the leaders of the next generation, children should be encouraged to be aware of specific measures they can exercise to keep the environment secure and clean for wildlife and people. They should also be encouraged to be safe, act responsibly, preserve the environment and always practice responsible outdoor behavior.

The Georgia Association of Broadcasters awarded "Boomer" the "Best Documentary" and "Best Television Series" in 1996 and 1997. Also in 1997, "Boomer" won his second Emmy Award for his work on "Sharks: Killers of the Caribbean. Fact or Fiction?" - collaborative videography. The Outdoor Writers Association of America (OWAA) gave "Boomer" four awards - two second place finishes and two for third place. The Southeastern Outdoor Press Association (SEOPA) judged "Boomer" as having the "Best Television Series".

"Boomer" was awarded "Excellence in Craft - Best of Class" by the Georgia Outdoor Writers Association (GOWA) in 1995. Additionally, there are several Addy awards that "Boomer" has won for his voice work on commercials.

SPENCER TURNER
Columbia, Missouri

Spencer Turner has fly fished from Maine to Washington, and from Alaska to Texas for the past 50-plus years. He was born in Northern Wisconsin and grew up on Rice Lake, a small flowage on the Red Cedar River, where he terrorized bluegills, crappie, bass and northern pike for more than 20 years. After acquiring a wife, family, a Bachelor's Degree in Conservation from the University of Wisconsin-Stevens Point, and a Master's Degree in Fisheries biology from Colorado State University, he joined the Missouri Department of Conservation as a fisheries biologist, the state's trout biologist, where he spent 29 years developing the state's nationally recognized modern trout program. He has received numerous local and national awards for his research and trout management efforts including the prestigious Professional Conservationist of the year award from Trout Unlimited.

Spencer's popular writing career blossomed in the 1980s in local and national magazines. He served as president of the Missouri Outdoor Communicators, board member for the 2,000 member Outdoor Writers Association of America, member of the American Fisheries Society, and member of the Embrace-A-Stream committee for Trout Unlimited. He has written hundreds of fishing and hunting articles and currently writes columns for "Midwest Fly Fisher," "Missouri Game and Fish," and the "Outdoor Guide." He shares his passion for fishing and hunting with his wife of 37 years, two cats, and 7 English Setters in his rural home near Columbia, Missouri.

BRENDA VALENTINE
Buchanan, Tennessee

Brenda Valentine, known as the "First Lady of Hunting," is recognized as one of the top women hunters and outdoor sports promoters in the world. A hunter since the age of four, she has been sharing her field experiences with television, radio and print audiences for the past 10 years. Additionally, she is a columnist and staff writer for "Bowhunter" magazine and a full-time freelance outdoor writer. Throughout the year Valentine educates and entertains live audiences with seminars and personal appearances at sport and outdoor shows nationwide. She is a member of Bass Pro Shops RedHead Pro Hunting Team, Bill Jordan's Realtree Team and Browning Archery Pro Staff. She endorses products made by Wildlife Research Center and Warren & Sweat Tree Stands.

Valentine has hunted throughout North America, Canada and Africa. She is skilled with all types of firearms including modern rifles, shotguns, handguns and muzzle loaders. Competitive tournament archery as well as bowhunting are both very strong suits of Brenda's.

Valentine was born and grew up in rural northwestern Tennessee where at an early age she was taught woodsmanship and field care of game meat. She draws upon a multitude of life experiences in the outdoors as she recruits new hunters, especially women and children. In addition to her enthusiastic promotion of hunting and the outdoors, she has been a very successful business owner, wife and mother and grandmother. Brenda considers the passing on of her knowledge and skills of the outdoors to be her greatest legacy.

JOEL VANCE
Jefferson City, Missouri

Joel Vance spent 22 years as an award-winning news and magazine writer for the Missouri Department of Conservation.

He has been a quail hunter for more than 40 years and has a new book, *Bobs, Brush and Brittanies,* on the market, along with two other books of humor and a book-on-tape of humor short stories. He believes implicitly that there are two times of the year: quail season and thinking about quail season.

Vance is now a full-time freelance writer, with four regular magazine columns as well as many articles. He is an Excellence in Craft honoree by the 2,000-member Outdoor Writers Association of America and has been awarded its top conservation communication honor. He also is a past president, two-time board member and board chairman of the group.

And he has six Brittanies and more shotguns than he needs, but not as many as he wants.

Vance's books: "Bobs, Brush and Brittanies" ($22) ; "Grandma and the Buck Deer" ($17); and "Confessions of an Outdoor Maladroit" ($22); available postpaid and autographed from Cedar Glade Press, Box 1664, Jefferson City, MO 65102.

RANDY VANCE
Ozark, Missouri

Randy Vance is an avid hunter and fisherman who resides in Ozark, Missouri. Presently the owner and president of Randy Vance Associates, a public relations and marketing firm, Randy has served firms such as MirrOlure, Star Rods, Honda Marine, Bass Pro Shops and many others. He has also spent more than 15 years as a free lance writer and photographer with credits in "Sports Afield," "Field & Stream," and "Better Homes and Gardens."

When fishing, his favorite quarry is snook and redfish in south Florida. Bonefish are close runners up. In the field, Randy's favorite game is sharptailed grouse and dumb, slow pheasants. He eats a lot of chicken. What little he learned about cooking, he learned from feeding himself, because few others who knew his sense of humor would join him at supper. Still, some have been surprised by his recipes contained in these pages and ate their results whether they were relatives or not.

MARK VAN PATTEN
Jefferson City, Missouri

Mark grew up on a Laclede County farm in south-central Missouri. He was raised by his grandparents who introduced him to the gentle art of fly fishing at a young age. With fly fishing came a deep and abiding passion for streams and their pristine beauty.

The Southern Council of the Federation of Fly Fishers named Mark "Conservationist of the Year" in 1990, and "Man of the Year" in 1991. Mark established Missouri's first STREAM TEAM, an "adopt a stream" program in 1988. His Team, the Roubidoux Fly Fishers Association, was presented with the STREAM TEAM Stewardship and Leadership awards in 1989 and 1990 respectively. In 1993, his STREAM TEAM was awarded the international "McKinnzie Cup" for stream conservation. Mark was individually presented with the "Award of Excellence" in 1992 by the Federation of Fly Fishers Southern Council, and "Educator of the Year," by the Roubidoux Fly Fishers Association in 1997. He served as President of the Southern Council of the Federation of Fly Fishers. He was presented with the "Arkansas Traveler," a commission as an ambassador to the state of Arkansas by the Governor, for helping Arkansas start their own STREAM TEAM program in 1997.

A published author, Mark served as President of the Missouri Outdoor Communicators and received a lifetime membership in 1997.

Mark worked for the Conservation Federation of Missouri as Missouri's STREAM TEAM Coordinator. The STREAM TEAM program received the National Wildlife Federation's prestigious, "Conservation Achievement Award" for education in 1997. Mark is now employed by the Missouri Department of Conservation as the Fisheries Coordination Biologist.

VIRGIL WARD
Amsterdam, Missouri

Virgil is best known for his "Championship Fishing" TV series for the past 20 years. In the early 1960s, Virgil was quite a renowned tournament angler. He won the World Series of Sport Fishing in 1962 and two national contests in 1964. He was elected to the National Fishing Hall of Fame. Virgil also taught fishing courses at Southwest Missouri State University. In the early 1940s, Virgil started Bass Buster Lure Company where he designed several lures and accessories such as his patented fiberguard weed guard. His "Championship Fishing" show has entertained millions of viewers over two decades.

Virgil contributed fishing columns to nearly 400 newspapers and did a radio show on approximately 250 stations. Virgil also authored a book, "Championship Fishing Guide". Among the celebrities he has filmed with are Hugh O'Brien, Nanette Fabray, Fred MacMurray, June Haver, Mel Tillis, Glenn Ford, Junior Samples, Marty Milner, Pete Rose, Darrell Porter and George Brett.

Virgil Ward is one of the real pioneers of television fishing shows. He has enjoyed success in all phases of the sport. He has entertained and educated men, women and children throughout the United States and Canada. He is a true legend of our great sport.

LARRY WEISHUHN
Uvalde, Texas

A native Texan, Larry started hunting with his dad, grandad and family while he was still in diapers. As a biologist he set up quality wildlife management programs on well over 12,000,000 acres across North America. As an award winning writer, he has authored well over 1,000 magazine features plus nearly as many columns. Currently he serves on staff with "Shooting Times," "Deer & Deer Hunting," "North American Hunter," "Outdoor World," "Texas Fish & Game," "Big Game Adventures," "Black Powder Hunting," and others. He is the editor of "Realtree Outdoors" and co-owns the Texas Hunting Directory. He has written numerous books and contributed chapters to many more. Larry has directed, produced, scripted and occasionally appeared in approximately 25 award winning outdoor videos. He frequently guests on national outdoor television shows, and serves as a featured speaker at national and international wildlife, hunting and management gatherings. Larry serves on the Pro Staffs of RedHead, Realtree and Hunter Specialties, Texas Seed Company, Trophy Xcellerator among others. Because of Larry's research, management, hunting and promotion of white-tailed deer he is frequently referred to in the national media as "Mr. Whitetail."

BOB WHITEHEAD
St. Louis, Missouri

A graduate of the University of Missouri - School of Journalism, Bob Whitehead has been involved in journalistic endeavors most of his career. The former St. Louis Globe Democrat Retail Advertising Manager currently serves as Managing Editor of "Outdoor Guide" magazine. He is editor of the Outdoor Sports section of the "St. Louis/Southern Illinois Labor Tribune" and hosts a weekly radio talk-show on the Big 550 KTRS St. Louis.

Bob is an active member of several outdoor writer groups including Outdoor Writers Association of America, AGLOW and MOC. Bob was the president of the Missouri Outdoor Communicators for 1999-2000.

LARRY WHITELEY
Springfield, Missouri

Larry has a deep love and appreciation for the great outdoors and a wealth of experience as well. He was editor of his very own outdoors newspaper for over five years and was host of his own outdoor TV show for three years. Larry has also had an outdoor radio show for over sixteen years and today can be heard in 48 states and 139 different foreign countries on "Bass Pro Shops Outdoor World" syndicated radio show.

Larry is an avid outdoorsman in just about all areas. He enjoys spending his spare time hunting, fishing, hiking and making nature furniture and crafts. Larry has always had a special place in his heart for children and enjoys spending time with youth and passing on his knowledge and experience to our next generation.

All of the following organizations support hunting and conservation. Consider joining one or more.

The Wilderness Society
900 17th Street, NW
Washington, DC 20006

The Izaak Walton League of
America
1401 Wilson Blvd., Level B
Arlington, VA 22209

The National Rifle Association of
America
1150 Waples Mill Road
Fairfax, VA 22030

Outdoor Writers Association of
America
2017 Cato Avenue, Suite 101
State College, PA 16801-2768

The Wildlife Legislative Fund of
America
50 West Broad Street
Columbus, OH 43215

Ducks Unlimited
National Headquarters
One Waterfowl Way
Memphis, TN 38120

The National Wildlife Federation
1400 Sixteenth Street, NW
Washington, DC 20036-2266

Wildlife Management Institute
1101 14th Street NW, Suite 801
Washington, DC 20005

The Wildlife Society
5410 Grosvenor Lane, Suite 200
Bethesda, MD 20814

Rocky Mountain Elk Foundation
P.O. Box 8249
Missoula, MT 59807-8249

National Shooting Sports
Foundation
Flintlock Ridge Office Center
11 Mile Hill Road
Newton, CT 06470-2359

The National Wild Turkey
Federation
P.O. Box 530
Edgefield, SC 29824

ODE TO A CAMPFIRE

I sit at your side and you warm me.
You soothe my aches and sweeten my senses.
Your glow mesmerizes and your crackle lulls me to sleep.
You are more than fire, you are friend.
You keep me company in the black of night.
You are my beacon in the wilderness.
Your sweet hickory breath saturates me.

I feed you sticks of strength.
You live through me and I through you.
Those who bask in your radiance are mellowed.
Oh, the tales you ignite and witness.
Your spirit ascends on a rising column of smoke.
And when you flicker and die, part of me dies too.
For your tongue is unique and gives special joy.
And when your final ember glows no more, I bid you farewell.

—Charlie Farmer

The best remedy for those who are afraid, lonely or unhappy is to go outside, somewhere where they can be quiet, alone with the heavens, nature and God. Because only then does one feel that all is as it should be and that God wishes to see people happy, amidst the simple beauty of nature. As long as this exists, and it certainly always will, I know that then there will always be comfort for every sorrow, whatever the circumstances may be. And I firmly believe that nature brings solace in all troubles.

—Anne Frank (1929–1945)
German Jewish refugee, diarist
"The Diary of a Young Girl"
Entry for 23 February, 1944

David Besenyer ©1998

BILL AND CHARLENE COOPER

AN INDIAN VERSION OF THE TWENTY-THIRD PSALM

Note: This beautiful Indian version originated many years ago with Arizona Indians who translated it into a universal sign language in order to share it with members of neighboring tribes who spoke different dialects. A white missionary then re-translated it into literal English—Indian style—which is as you see it here.

The Great Father above a shepherd Chief is. I am His and with Him I want not. He throws out to me a rope and the name of the rope is love and He draws me to where the grass is green and the water not dangerous, and I eat and lie down and am satisfied. Sometimes my heart is very weak and falls down but He lifts me up again and draws me into a good road. His name is WONDERFUL.

Sometime, it may be very soon, it may be a long, long time, He will draw me into a valley. It is dark there, but I'll be afraid not, for it is in between those mountains that the Shepherd Chief will meet me and the hunger that I have in my heart all through this life will be satisfied.

Sometimes He makes the love rope into a whip, but afterwards He gives me a staff to lean upon. He spreads a table before me with all kinds of foods. He puts His hand upon my head and all the "tired" is gone. My cup He fills till it runs over. What I tell is true. I lie not. These roads that are "away ahead" will stay with me through this life and after; and afterwards I will go to live in the Big Tepee and sit down with the SHEPHERD CHIEF forever.

Index

253

S

SALADS

SAUCES & GRAVIES

SEAFOOD

Crabmeat

Shrimp

SMALL GAME

U

UPLAND GAME

Billie R. Cooper
Outdoor Celebrities Cookbook
19255 St. Rt. EE
St. James, MO 65559

Please send_____copy(ies)   @ $21.95 each _____
    Postage and handling   @ $ 3.00 each _____
    Missouri residents add sales tax   @ $ 1.37 each _____
                                                  Total   _____

Name_____
Address_____
City_____ State_____ Zip_____

    Make checks payable to Dry Creek Press

Billie R. Cooper
Outdoor Celebrities Cookbook
19255 St. Rt. EE
St. James, MO 65559

Please send_____copy(ies)   @ $21.95 each _____
    Postage and handling   @ $ 3.00 each _____
    Missouri residents add sales tax   @ $ 1.37 each _____
                                                  Total   _____

Name_____
Address_____
City_____ State_____ Zip_____

    Make checks payable to Dry Creek Press

Billie R. Cooper
Outdoor Celebrities Cookbook
19255 St. Rt. EE
St. James, MO 65559

Please send_____copy(ies)   @ $21.95 each _____
    Postage and handling   @ $ 3.00 each _____
    Missouri residents add sales tax   @ $ 1.37 each _____
                                                  Total   _____

Name_____
Address_____
City_____ State_____ Zip_____

    Make checks payable to Dry Creek Press

Apache™ Sport Boats

True tested on the Mississippi Flyway. The unique hull and floatation design makes this boat virtually untippable. Feel secure in any water or weather conditions. Custom colors or 3 camouflage patterns.

SportBox™

Fits all receiver hitches. Heavy duty, but lightweight. The ideal way to expand the use of your vehicle. Custom colors.

FiberLite™ Dog Kennels

Safe and comfortable transportation for the Sportsman's hunting breeds, or the family pet. Custom colors or 3 camouflage patterns.

For More Details Call:
1-800-536-4604

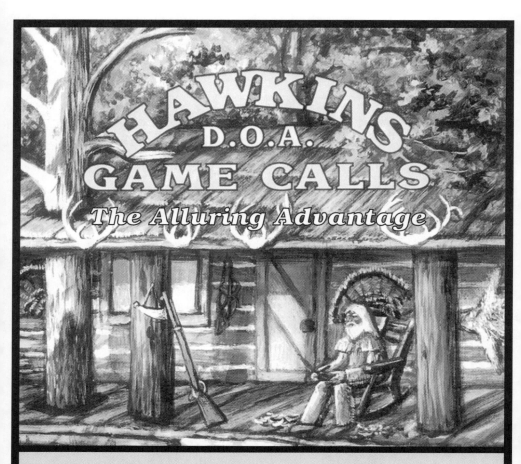

Rafter Ⱥ Ranch

Professional Guided Deer & Turkey Hunting

The Rafter A Ranch

9330 Hwy. E
Houston, MO 65483
417-967-3519
jgabel@train.missouri.org
Freddie, Pat & Justin Adey

Rafter A Ranch owner Freddie Adey offers helpful advice to professional hunter Alex Rutledge and outdoor writers/photographers Bill & Charlene Cooper.

Rafter A Ranch consists of over 2,000 acres of spectacular beauty in the heart of the Missouri Ozarks in Texas County. Hardwood ridges, Big Piney River bottoms, agricultural fields, and food plots interspersed throughout Rafter A make it a prime hunting spot for trophy class whitetail deer, wild turkey and small game.

A remote, rustic lodge complements the wild atmosphere at Rafter A. Charming decor, clean facilities, hot showers and fabulous home-cooked meals soothe body and soul after a day of hunting. Quiet luxury and warm hospitality are the trademarks of owners Pat, Freddie and Justin Adey.

As an outdoor writer and outdoor radio program host, I highly recommend Rafter A Ranch.

—Bill Cooper

★ FISHING ★ HUNTING ★ BOATING ★ CAMPING

Subscribe Today —
6 BIG ISSUES
For Only $8~~95~~ $8~~00~~

Outdoor Guide Magazine Will Send a Greeting (from the Editor) for Each Gift Subscription Order.

For A FREE Copy of the Magazine Call 1-800-706-2444

Make Check or Money Order Payable to: **OUTDOOR GUIDE**

Mail to: **OUTDOOR GUIDE MAGAZINE**
505 South Ewing Avenue, St. Louis, Missouri 63103

YES!	Please Start My One-Year Subscription	— GIFT SUBSCRIPTION FORM — Order as Many as You Like!

Name _____

Address _____

City _____

State _____

Zip _____

Name _____

Address _____

City _____

State _____

Zip _____